BITING the BULLET

BITING the BULLET

~Memoirs of a Police Officer~

AJAI RAJ SHARMA

RUPA

Published by
Rupa Publications India Pvt. Ltd 2020
7/16, Ansari Road, Daryaganj
New Delhi 110002

Sales Centres:
Allahabad Bengaluru Chennai
Hyderabad Jaipur Kathmandu
Kolkata Mumbai

Copyright © Ajai Raj Sharma 2020

The views and opinions expressed in this book are the author's own and the facts are as reported by him which have been verified to the extent possible, and the publishers are not in any way liable for the same.

All rights reserved.
No part of this publication may be reproduced, transmitted, or stored in a retrieval system, in any form or by any means, electronic, mechanical, photocopying, recording or otherwise, without the prior permission of the publisher.

ISBN: 978-93-5333-777-3

First impression 2020

10 9 8 7 6 5 4 3 2 1

Printed at Parksons Graphics Pvt. Ltd, Mumbai

The moral right of the author has been asserted.

This book is sold subject to the condition that it shall not, by way of trade or otherwise, be lent, resold, hired out, or otherwise circulated, without the publisher's prior consent, in any form of binding or cover other than that in which it is published.

*In the memory of my parents,
my father, the late Indra Raj Sharma, and
my mother, the late Umeshwari Sharma.*

CONTENTS

Introduction   ix

1. My Career Begins   1
2. Bareilly and the Saga of Omkar Singh Yadav   13
3. The Dacoits of Agra   26
4. Banaras: A Tricky Terrain   50
5. Banda: The Wild West   58
6. Crime Capital, Farrukhabad   74
7. The Rise and Fall of Jarman Singh   85
8. The Dreaded Gangster Sheodan Kachhi   103
9. Special Task Force and the Killing of Sriprakash Shukla   127
10. My Days with Delhi Police   145
11. The Valiant and Versatile Border Security Force   168

Epilogue   181
Acknowledgements   185

INTRODUCTION

There is no limit to the good a man can do, if he doesn't care who gets the credit.

—Benjamin Jowett

'Cut to the chase.' This phrase which dates back to Hollywood Westerns from the early 1930s has defined and governed my life in police. As children, we wanted to fast-forward all that boring dialogue and quickly get to those thrilling scenes in which the good guys mounted their horses to chase armed bandits across the desert. Over the years, this phrase has travelled from Hollywood to other parts of the world. I must confess with equal measure of pride and achievement, that my policing years have seen both the 'chasing of the bandits' and 'coming to the point'.

This book is a retelling of the life in khaki that I have proudly lived for more than four decades. I think of it more as a memoir than an autobiography, a chronicle of some of the best, most exciting and challenging adventures that I have had in uniform, chasing bandits, tracing terrorists, quenching communal fires, unearthing match-fixing syndicates and much more. After having served in the coveted Indian Police Service (IPS) for more than thirty-eight years and being in action for the most part of my professional life, writing about them feels surreal. For even though I am sitting in my quiet study, I feel like I can still hear the sharp crack of gunshots, the clap of hooves in the ravines of the Chambal, the sound of my own breath as I chase a dreaded dacoit through tall fields of sugarcane. I recall the complex circles of informers, the interrogations, nabbing criminals, and of course, the much maligned 'encounters' I've had. This is the life I have lived, and this memoir is a tribute to those moments that have brought me bouquets and brickbats at the same time.

How does one judge how good a police officer is? Is a good officer the one who always follows the rule book even if it means letting go of the criminal? Or is he or she the one who makes their own rules, who thinks nothing of bringing criminals and outlaws to justice, even if it means deviating from that rule book? There is no right or wrong answer. Most police officers operate in, what can be called, a vast expanse of grey area. Thus, for me, a good police officer is one who brings the culprit to the book, without jeopardizing his conscience. This might sound strange coming from a police officer who has been known to devise his own means and methods to nab criminals. However, my conscience has always been my guiding star. Some people have called

Biting the Bullet

me an 'encounter specialist' but believe me, this is a term I detest. For me, it is no badge of honour and, in fact, the usage of the term is flawed. Others, especially some friends in the media, nicknamed me 'Dirty Harry', knowing my record of eliminating criminals. Honestly, this does not give me a high either; never has and never will. All I have done is reacted to a situation, devised my plans, motivated the bunch of officers working under me and with me and got the job done. After all, someone has to get his hands dirty to clear the filth. If that makes Harry dirty, so be it.

I have been fortunate in my career that some of the most high profile cases came on my radar, and I was able to deliver them successfully. The 2001 December Parliament attack, the match-fixing scandal, the terrorist attack at the Red Fort, the formation of the Special Task Force (STF) and killing of Sriprakash Shukla—these are some of the cases that come to mind, when people talk about me. Over the past few years, they have defined me, and the common comment when people see me is, 'Oh! This is Ajai Raj Sharma of the Parliament attack case!' or, 'Oh, so you are that Ajai Raj Sharma who created the STF and eliminated Sriprakash Shukla!' These definitely are some of the most famous and high-profile cases that were sensational at the time they occurred, but these are just a part of my career, albeit an exciting part. These cases do feature prominently in the book, but I will take my readers further back in time and tell stories that served as my training ground, cases that baptized me, that made me. Stories of dacoits and banditry, of the rustic terrains of Chambal and Farrukhabad, of gangsters (and unlike what they show in Bollywood films, dacoits don't use horses!) and their paramours, of the deceptive world of informers and brutal killings and of coming face-to-face with a dreaded dacoit of Chambal and negotiating with him, I started my career in these Badlands and the time has now come to take you through my journey.

My policing journey began in Agra when, as a young IPS officer, freshly minted from the academy, I was asked to serve in the rough terrains of Uttar Pradesh's (UP) proverbial Wild West. For a complete greenhorn to be thrown in the area infested with dacoits, it was overwhelming. I could have failed by the sheer prospect of locking horns with the outlaws who would not think twice before firing. But I told myself that perhaps I was being chosen for this to prepare myself for various challenges in future. This was proved right.

They say that as a police officer, you never quite get over that first encounter with death, which is why, although I have seen more than my fair share of bloodshed, violence and death over the years, I'll never forget the face of Sub-inspector (SI) Mahavir Singh who was shot dead by dreaded dacoits during my first posting in Agra. If Mahavir Singh's saga is that of an honest police inspector laying down his life for duty, Omkar Singh Yadav's tale is no less dramatic than a Bollywood film. Here was a uniformed man, who was so wronged in life that he took to the gun! The dreaded Sheodan Kachhi's story is even bloodier—he would sadistically make his victim's family members dance over the victim's corpse! I've often said a thriller should be made on his rise and

Biting the Bullet

ultimate fall. I hear that a film is being made on him right now and this vindicates my point.

These characters have stayed with me throughout my life. Some still make me recoil with horror, others with sadness. I remember how we cultivated a criminal as an informer. He was planted in a gang as our mole. He gave us very good intelligence that eventually helped us to neutralize the gang. But the script of life does not necessarily have a happy ending. My informer had to pay for his efforts with his life. In modern parlance, it is called collateral damage, but I still feel the pain of losing him after so many years. In modern times, personnel serving in the force are provided with counselling sessions to counter post-traumatic stress disorder, but during the 1960s and 1970s, such practices were unheard of. An officer had to bear and live with his pain and find ways to overcome it himself.

These days, we live in tech-savvy times. Everyone is connected, and information and misinformation reach their destination at the same time. With WhatsApp, Facebook, Twitter, emails and other modes of online communication, messages are conveyed instantly. We are so used to this life that thinking about a wireless life seems impossible. And I would request my readers to bear in mind that during most of my early career, there were no mobiles, no emails, no WhatsApp... It is perhaps hard to even imagine today that it used to take days, weeks and sometimes months for my informers to provide me information about criminals. Sometimes, I was told to reach a particular spot within hours of the information being provided to catch the goon, and that particular spot could be forty to fifty kilometres from where I was. In one of the cases, I had to walk, cross a river in a bullock cart and then reach a spot where the dacoit had been hiding. And mind you, the dacoit was caught alive and produced in court taking the same route back!

I must take refuge in the timeless cliché that there never was a dull moment in my career. If the ravines of Chambal literally made me run through the terrain, sometimes in jeeps and often on foot, the posting in districts of Agra, Bareilly, Benares (Varanasi), Banda, Farrukhabad, Aligarh, Allahabad (now Prayagraj), Meerut and Lucknow made me realize the significance of administering big districts. Some of these districts were politically significant while some were communally sensitive. In short, the police administration was often sitting on a tinderbox. For instance, I still remember that after controlling a communal riot in Varanasi, I was summoned by the chief minister (CM), Shri Kamalapati Tripathi at the time, himself a local. He was sitting on the floor and taking minute details from me about the riot which had recently taken place while his attendant was giving him a shave. And after some time, the then prime minister, Indira Gandhi, telephoned him asking for my suspension, as I had taken strong action to control the riot in the CM's constituency.

However, the CM knew that I had taken the right action under the given circumstances, and he defended me in front of the mighty Indira Gandhi. Consequently, an enquiry was ordered, and I came out clean. I often wonder how far

Biting the Bullet

politicians would go today to support a young IPS officer and, that too, against the wishes of the prime minister of the country.

After dealing with such political ramifications of curbing a communal riot, my next posting was to a district where crime was an institution. The undeveloped and crime-infested Banda district posed a different challenge. Every crime that took place there was seen through the lens of caste, and hence in a caste-driven society and a political place like UP, it added even more trouble for the administration. This stint prepared me for my next posting to Farrukhabad, stronghold of dreaded dacoits Sheodan Kaachi and Jarman Singh. After ending their reign of terror, I moved to Aligarh, which, again, was a communally sensitive district. Communal flare-ups were common and resorting to a lathi charge or firing was the option best not exercised. Aligarh taught me the importance of communicating with the civil society and winning their confidence. It was there that I discovered an effective way to win over local youngsters of Aligarh—through sports.

My posting as the senior superintendent of police (SSP) of Allahabad was a homecoming for me. I was returning to the city of my alma mater. I had studied in Boys' High School for some years and after that, I had done my graduation from Ewing Christian College and post-graduation from the University of Allahabad. This was a city where I had spent my youth, this was where I had dreamt of becoming an IPS officer, and this was where I had fulfilled that dream. Allahabad was always a politically and administratively very important district and helming the police affairs there was an enriching experience. It did not have as many instances of crime as Banda or Farrukhabad, but it was a big district with a modern outlook. A city rich in culture and literature, it did have its share of criminals and outlaws. The Bhukkal Maula gang and their exploits is now part of its urban folklore. That this gang was not only controlled but also curbed when Bhukkal surrendered before me, is one of my success stories.

Meerut was another district that had both political and administrative challenges. It also was a district where a substantial number of communal riots had taken place since independence and hence had to be dealt with caution and firmness at the same time. Another challenging district for me was Agra, where I had already served in two different capacities. A third posting in Agra as its senior superintendent of Police (SSP) proved lucky for me. It was here that I got my second President's Police Medal for Gallantry (BAR) for liquidating the notorious Jagta Kachhi gang. By this time, my exploits had been well documented by my superiors as well as the media. I remember I was reluctant to take on the job of additional director general (law and order) in Lucknow, but when CM Kalyan Singh told me about the menace of Sriprakash Shukla and how he had taken a *supari* (the money paid to a hitman) of five crore rupees to assassinate him, I had no option but to take on the responsibility. As a result, the Special Task Force was born.

Memory takes me back to the time when I was appointed

commissioner of police, Delhi. It was the most unusual posting of my life simply because I belonged to the Uttar Pradesh cadre and not to the Union Territories (UT) cadre. As such, I had been labelled an outsider in Delhi. I still remember my first press conference where some not-so-friendly members of the press asked me how I would control crime if I did not even know where the thanas of Delhi were geographically located. My answer to them was simple: 'I have the knowledge of the Indian Penal Code and the other essential laws, and this is all I need to know to perform my duties as a commissioner.' Looking back in time, I can say that I have not done badly either.

This memoir is a recollection of events that have shaped my professional journey. Some names have been changed to protect their identity, since they have been my informers, and for some, a generation has gone by, and it would not be fair to their children and grandchildren to see them in a bad light. I strongly believe that this memoir can also serve as a document for young police officers to learn how, even with a lack of resources, one can successfully perform his or her duty, if the intent is right. I have tried to be as true to the events as possible, by speaking to the people who were there at the time and by relying on my journal of entries that I have maintained. I now leave it to the wisdom of my readers to read my story and see for themselves my life in uniform.

And now, without wasting any time, let's 'cut to the chase'.

1
MY CAREER BEGINS

As a student, I had studied that Agra, home to the Taj Mahal, had been founded by Sikandar Lodi and later ruled by successive Mughal rulers, from Babur to Shah Jahan. As a freshly minted IPS officer, I was told that this was the city I was to cut my professional teeth in. Having completed rounds of rigorous training in Mussoorie, Mount Abu and finally at the Police Training College (PTC) in Moradabad, which was an introduction to the UP Police, I thought I was well prepared. How wrong I was!

For within days of arriving in Agra, I realized that there was one aspect of the city, which historians and cultural analysts had failed to capture. Through the lens of a police officer, there was only one thing that Agra was famous, or should I say infamous, for. And this was its long and hallowed tradition of banditry.

Ajai Raj Sharma

THE DREADED DACOITS OF CHAMBAL

Located in and around the ravines of Chambal, Agra has produced some of the most dreaded dacoits of the nineteenth and the twentieth centuries in India. Dacoits of yesteryears preferred being called *baaghi*s (rebels) instead of 'dakoos'. They felt that they were up against an exploitative social and political order. Soon after independence, as the country moved towards the socialist model, the zamindars, or landowners, found themselves on the wrong side of the government. The rural population now had expectations of a better future for themselves. Sadly, this did not happen. The ravines of Chambal thus continued to turn disgruntled youths into dacoits.

When I took charge as assistant superintendent of police (ASP) in Agra, I was fortunate to work under S.K. Shunglu, one of the finest officers one could have as a mentor to launch one's career as an IPS. He was the SSP of Agra, a significant district posting in the state. Initially, my job was to shadow the SSP to observe how he went about the daily business of maintaining law and order and administering his force. Invariably, most of his day went in addressing the complaints of the large numbers of people who would throng his office. Most of the time, their complaints had to do with the fact that they had registered First Information Reports (FIRs) but no progress had been made on their cases. Some complaints were related to corruption within the police department while others were regarding the police favouring a particular party or a person.

Biting the Bullet

One morning, it was business as usual at the SSP's office. I was sitting behind him, observing him dealing with complainants from various parts of Agra district with his usual good humour and efficiency. All of a sudden, the SSP received a crash wireless message that left us dumbfounded. Thirty children, along with their class teacher, had been kidnapped from the classroom of a school in Kheragarh!

THE CRIME THAT SHOOK AGRA

All the children in a class abducted! This was a sensational crime. The news that followed was even more sensational. Forty armed gangsters, belonging to the notorious gang of Phoola, had hijacked a bus at gunpoint, shot dead the station officer of Kheragarh police station and escaped with the children and their teacher in it.

This message completely rattled the SSP. He immediately got up from his chair and said, 'I have never heard of such a crime. Let's go!' As we left for the crime scene, I kept wondering why the dacoits would kidnap an entire classroom. Meanwhile, the SSP gave me the background of the Janga-Phoola gang, which had been plundering the district of Agra over a decade. Their story was now folklore in the whole Chambal region.

Phoola belonged to a village called Bajna, in the Rajakhera area of Bharatpur district in Rajasthan. Bajna was located close to the border of Agra district. He joined the gang of Janga, which used to operate on a simple age-old principle, *'Riyasat mein raho aur Angrezee ko looto'* (live in the erstwhile princely states of the British Raj and loot the areas ruled by the British in UP). The practice of gangs like this one, was to take shelter in states like Dholpur and Bharatpur, which belonged to Maharajas and Rajas, and in lieu of this, the dacoits committed no crime in their jurisdiction. Instead, they looted and plundered areas belonging to the United Provinces ruled by the British, which meant that their area of operation now was Agra district. After Janga, Phoola had become the leader of the gang. He took his depredations to a much higher level of menace. He greatly improved the weaponry of his gang, outfitting them with sophisticated firearms such as semi-automatic rifles and sten guns. What was more, years of operating with impunity had made the gang arrogant as well as bloodthirsty, which did not augur well for the general populace as well as for the keepers of law and order of the area.

◆

A crowd had already gathered at the crime scene when we reached it. The body of SI Mahavir Singh, who was the station officer of the Kheragarh police station, lay riddled with bullets in a pool of blood. His right hand was gripping a strap that had 'Kunwarji Gadaria' written on it. We were informed that the gang had come to specifically kidnap two boys, belonging to affluent families. However, when the dacoits reached their school, they could not identify their targets. So they decided to abduct the entire class. Before

Biting the Bullet

leaving the school, Phoola had announced that he would release the others after identifying the boys.

Obviously, even for a powerful gang like theirs, it was not practical to kidnap so many children and then expect to hike with them to a secure spot, without attracting attention! Hijacking a bus from the highway was an obvious solution.

The dacoits stopped the first bus they saw coming their way and asked all the passengers to get off. The passengers were terrified at the sight of the armed gangsters. A frantic Phoola shouted that if the passengers did not hurry, he would start shooting them down one by one. SI Mahavir Singh was among the passengers on that bus. He instructed the passengers to remain seated, got off the bus and told the gangsters that nobody would be getting off. Phoola was shocked that someone had the temerity to challenge his orders.

'Are you mad? Nobody disobeys my orders!' Phoola screamed at him angrily. 'Don't you know who I am? I am the dreaded Phoola of Bajna.'

'Of course, I know who you are,' replied Mahavir Singh. 'But I want to know why you are doing this.'

'And who are you?' questioned Phoola, a little perplexed.

'I am Mahavir Singh, the station officer of Kheragarh police station, and I have asked the passengers not to get down from the bus,' he said.

The terrified passengers listened to this exchange of words with bated breath. Phoola was taken aback by Mahavir's courage.

'You are brave all right, but very stupid for defying me,'

he told Mahavir Singh. 'Get out of my way, and don't stop the passengers from getting off the bus!'

But Mahavir Singh again ordered the passengers to stay inside the bus, knowing this was the only way to stall the gang from decamping with the children. Phoola was flabbergasted at his stubbornness. He asked him, 'Do you think you can stop us from doing what we came here to do? Do you think you can kill me?'

Mahavir replied, 'Of course, I can kill you. Unfortunately, I am unarmed, or else you would have been dead by now.'

Phoola was already fuming. He had never been defied or challenged in this manner publicly. He shouted at Mahavir Singh, 'Enough is enough. Get out of our way or else you will be killed.'

Mahavir replied, 'I am the station officer of this area. I will not allow you to commit any crime in my presence.'

This was the last straw. Phoola asked one of the members of the gang, Gullo, who was the only female amongst them, to fire at Mahavir Singh. And Gullo shot him dead.

Who was Gullo and why had Phoola chosen her to kill Mahavir Singh?

Gullo was the paramour of Phoola. Their love story was born in the rugged terrains of a tiny and nondescript village of the erstwhile Bharatpur district. She was a young and sprightly woman. She was agile and full of youthful exuberance, one who expected a lot from the future. Much to her disgust, she was married to someone more than twice her age. He was addicted to smoking tobacco. His best way to pass time was to sit on the wall of the village

Biting the Bullet

well and smoke a hookah. Gullo and her husband were a total mismatch, which, naturally, made her unhappy in her marriage.

Phoola used to visit her village frequently. It was a matter of time before the dacoit and the dissatisfied wife became lovers. Gullo felt suffocated in her marriage with the old man and decided to get rid of him. Back in those days, nobody went to the court to seek a divorce. She had only one option.

She killed him.

One day, her husband was sitting on the wall of the well, smoking his hookah. No one was around. Gullo stealthily crept up behind him and pushed him into the well. The merry widow had eloped with Phoola even before her unfortunate husband's body could be pulled out.

Gullo was now part of the Phoola gang and accompanied them everywhere they went. Phoola taught her how to hold a rifle and how to fire it. However, there was one thing about Gullo that kept worrying him. She was the only member of the gang who was not a wanted criminal, and as far as the police was concerned, she had a clean record. He felt that her clean record was a great danger to the gang. He eagerly wanted Gullo to commit a crime.

Standing unarmed before the gang on that fateful day, Mahavir Singh provided Phoola with the opportunity he had been waiting for. He said to Gullo, 'Prove your loyalty by shooting Mahavir Singh dead.'

Mahavir Singh realized his last moment had come. He saw Kunwarji Gadaria standing next to Gullo. He desperately tried to snatch the rifle from Gadaria, but Gadaria was too quick for him. He caught hold of Mahavir's hands. Mahavir grabbed onto the leather strap containing bullets that Gadaria had hung across his chest. In the melee that ensued, a dacoit hit Mahavir on his head with the butt of his rifle. Mahavir fell to the ground still clutching Gadaria's strap. Finally, Gullo shot a burst of bullets at Mahavir from a semi-automatic rifle, killing him instantly. The gang immediately left in the bus with the kidnapped children.

When the SSP and I reached the crime scene, we saw the lifeless body of Mahavir Singh with gaping bullet holes, lying on the ground. After hearing the account of eyewitnesses of the brutal murder and the courage and doggedness he had displayed, I was deeply moved. Even years after my retirement today, whenever I am reminded of that dastardly crime, the still body of the brave Mahavir Singh comes to my mind and my eyes well up with tears.

The SSP was equally disturbed by the heinousness of the crime. He immediately ordered the circle officer of Kheragarh to start tracking the gang and try establishing contact with them to get the children back. Additional Provincial Armed Constabulary (PAC) companies were placed at his disposal. There was little else left for us to do but depart for Agra with heavy hearts. The kidnapped children returned one by one. Only the two boys, who Phoola wanted to kidnap for ransom, were held back, and they were released when their parents paid him the ransom money.

I was seething at the audacity of the gang. How I wished that I could get a chance to go after the Phoola gang and

Biting the Bullet

avenge the killing of Mahavir Singh! But of course, there was no way I could get such an opportunity, since I was in my probation period. Little did I know then, that years later, I would get my chance to bring that entire gang to justice and avenge Mahavir Singh's death. But that's a story for another chapter.

For the moment, my first encounter with Phoola and his misdeeds taught me that it isn't always, or even often, that the police is able to close a case immediately after the crime has taken place. In fact, against such gangs, the police is always at a disadvantage. Whenever the police has to confront them on their own turf, the police will usually find itself on the losing side, due to all the local advantages being with the gang. So I carried the burden of not having apprehended the wrongdoers in this crime and continued with my training. Week after week, a routine procedure followed—parades, inspections, visiting rural and urban police stations and more. Towards the end of my eight-month training, I gained valuable experience in the rural areas of Agra district. It was during this training that I was located in Bah (an area in the Chambal ravines), where I got to know about Man Singh and some other very notorious dacoits of yesteryears and their exploits. Man Singh was the one who had eluded the police for a very long time.

THE ROBIN HOOD OF THE CHAMBAL RAVINES

Man Singh belonged to Pinahat village in the sub-division of Bah, deep in the ravines of the Chambal. He had become a *baaghi* over a land dispute in which he felt grave injustice had been done to his family. Although he had a powerful gang of about fifty to sixty gangsters, all armed with sophisticated weaponry, he never allowed them to ill-treat the elderly, women or children. In fact, legend had it that he always helped the poor and the needy financially and helped many poor families get their daughters married. The local populace revered him as a kind of Robin Hood and affectionately referred to him as *Dau* (an elderly figure). As a result, the police could not get any information about him, and he and his gang survived for a long time.

Man Singh had five sons, all famous dacoits. His favourite son, Roopa, was also ironically, adopted. His biological father was Man Singh's *purohit* (priest). When the old priest was dying, he handed over Roopa's custody to Man Singh. Thus, a boy who was born in a priest's family was brought up by dacoits and grew up to become a dreaded bandit.

Roopa carried out a number of daring strikes. When a detachment of the Special Armed Force (SAF) of the Madhya Pradesh Police finally surrounded Man Singh and killed him, Roopa vowed to not allow the police to cremate him. He, along with his men, waged a grim battle with the SAF troops, who ultimately succeeded in taking Man Singh's dead body to the district headquarters.

Roopa succeeded Man Singh and turned out to be a very able gang leader. Later, his rivalry with the gang of Lakhan Singh, alias Laakhan, became legendary. The growing economic inequality in this region later led to the spurt of many notorious dacoits such as Mohar Singh, Nathu Singh, Madho Singh and, of course, Malkhan Singh, who gave himself the title of *Dasyu Samrat*, king of the dacoits.

I joined Bah in the month of May for my attachment training. Bah is one of the hottest places in the country. In summer, the mercury sometimes rises to 50 degrees! There was no accommodation available there for me, so I had to live in the police station. It didn't even have an electricity connection. Moreover, Bah has an inhospitable terrain. Unlike the police, the dacoits were used to the terrain as well as the climate. They would crisscross the ravines on foot in the blazing hot sun, secure in the knowledge that few would be foolish enough to pursue them, especially when they could so easily sneak across the border into Madhya Pradesh and return back at will.

All the gangs in the area had been assigned code names. Whenever a gang crossed the Chambal, the information was sent by a wireless message to all police stations on the other side, using the code of that gang. Whenever such a message was received, the usual drill was that all police stations concerned would lay an ambush on the likely routes that the gang could supposedly take. Most of the times, the ambush lasted for four to five hours. It got particularly difficult during peak summers when the sand would be burning and the police had to wait for the gang for hours lying on burning sand.

During my attachment in Bah, I had to lay such traps on several occasions. We would lie in the scorching heat on the burning sand in wait for the dacoits. On two occasions, we exchanged fire but were not successful in nabbing or killing any dacoit. These experiences were very difficult but proved invaluable for me in my later career.

Meanwhile, my probation was coming to an end and I already felt battle-hardened after Bah. How I wished that my first regular posting would be in Agra itself! But that was not to be.

Instead, I was posted to Bareilly.

2
BAREILLY AND THE SAGA OF OMKAR SINGH YADAV

All I knew about Bareilly when I was posted there as the ASP at the end of December 1968 was that it was in Uttar Pradesh and was famous for the manufacture of furniture. An SSP headed Bareilly Police, and the deputy inspector general of police (DIG) was also stationed there. When I reported my arrival to the SSP, I was in for a disappointment. He told me that a senior ASP was already posted there, and I would not get a circle to head immediately. I had been looking forward to put all my training, especially all that I had learnt in Agra, into practice. For I had heard that this was the period where an officer learnt the practical nitty-gritty of how to police a district.

Since there was no independent office for me, I was asked to operate from the main police station of Bareilly city, which was a hub for all activities in the city. The SSP suggested that I should look after agitations and processions which were a regular phenomenon in the city area. If this wasn't disappointing enough, I discovered that not only would I not get an official accommodation for the time being (the senior ASP was staying in the designated house) but that the leave I had applied for would not be sanctioned! This was crushing as I'd applied for leave to get married; all the arrangements had been made, the invitations had been sent out and the marriage was impossible to postpone. So my first few days in Bareilly were spent pleading for leave instead of studying my area of work! Eventually, the SSP of Bareilly agreed to grant me ten days' leave. It was hardly enough but I would have to do with it.

When I returned to Bareilly with my wife, we faced serious problems in getting accommodation. The city police officers were able to somehow manage a fairly big room in the Rifle Club. We used the room as our bedroom and enclosed one end of the veranda with a tent to use as a makeshift kitchen. I mention these problems not just because they happened to me, but because such infrastructural issues and lack of adequate leave remain problems that young police officers continue to face even today.

MY FIRST SUCCESSFUL CASE

Since I had to sit in the office of the circle officer of Bareilly city, which was located at the police station Kotwali, I could get an insider's perspective on how police matters were dealt with in an urban setting. The CO, Bhupender Singh, was an amiable man, a very experienced and shrewd person in his job. Whenever I wasn't managing processions and agitations, I would be at the police station, where people would come to report cases and lodge FIRs.

One evening, a man rushed in, crying. He had been robbed of all his money and wanted to file a report. However, instead of writing an FIR, the head constable started shouting at him and asked for his details. The complainant said he was Chandan Singh from Almora district.

'My daughter is getting married next month. I had come to Bareilly with ten thousand rupees to make some purchases for her marriage,' he said. 'I had gone to a *dhaba* to have food and was robbed of all my money! Now I don't have enough for a ticket to go home...'

The unsympathetic head constable shouted at Chandan Singh: 'First you blow up your money on alcohol, and now you have come to the police station to file a fake report of robbery!' Poor Chandan Singh started weeping. If his FIR couldn't be lodged, would the head constable just loan him money to go home, he asked?

The head constable's behaviour was highly objectionable. He was treating the victim like a criminal! I reasoned with him but to no avail. So I requested him to detail two constables with canes with me so that I could examine the facts myself. So we went to the *dhaba* where the robbery had occurred, in my private car (I did not have one allotted by the government). Chandan Singh recognized two people inside. They were the persons who probably had committed the crime. We moved in swiftly and took them by surprise. Within minutes, we ascertained that they weren't hardened criminals but just guys who had seized the opportunity for a quick buck. They had got Chandan Singh drunk till he passed out and then robbed him of his money and wrist watch. Chandan Singh, the two constables and the two goons piled into my car, and I drove them back to the Kotwali police station.

When we returned, the head constable did not know where to look! This was the first case I solved single-handedly. My experiment taught me that prompt action by the police could crack a case with ease. I got similar success in two or three more cases.

Before long, the local press got wind of my work and began to mention me in their columns almost daily. A prominent local newspaper, *Bareilly Samachar*, carried the headline, *'Nav Yuvak ASP ka Apraadh Virodhi Jihad'* (A Young ASP's Jihad against Crime). The Range DIG also expressed his appreciation but asked what the other officers had been doing till then. This made me feel awkward as most of my colleagues had been nothing but kind to me.

GAINING THE PUBLIC'S TRUST

The prevailing situation also created problems for me personally. Many complainants had begun to visit my residence at odd hours. One night, a few hours post-midnight, the bell rang. Two agitated men were at my door,

Biting the Bullet

asking for my help. Apparently, miscreants had vandalized a Shiva temple in Shayamatganj and tempers were running high. They were worried that a riot was imminent.

I didn't have the requisite status as a police officer to act on this alarming information, neither did I have a vehicle or policemen at my disposal. But how could I ignore it? So I apprised the SSP and the Inspector Baradari in whose jurisdiction the temple was located. Then, I bundled the two informants into my own car and drove to the scene. An agitated crowd had gathered there, shouting provocative slogans. The SSP and the Inspector soon arrived with a force. Together we appeased the angry mob, saying that the dignity of the temple would soon be restored and the culprits apprehended. Finally, the mob dispersed.

After normalcy had been restored, the SSP met all the police officers at the police station. He congratulated me, in particular, for my role, and expressed surprise at how I had managed to win the confidence of the people to the extent that, instead of reporting crime at the police station, they preferred to reach out to me directly. Perhaps they came to me because I empathized with their plight, I mused. This attitude stood me in good stead right till the end of my career in the police.

Meanwhile, the senior ASP was promoted to SP, and I finally got my chance to supervise a regular circle consisting of four police stations and the police lines, from where the entire force of the district is administered. I was allotted the ASP's official residence and an additional allowance of fifty rupees per month, which, in those days, was a lot of money. I was finally a full-fledged police officer and had realized my childhood dream.

THE HIGHWAY ROBBERS OF BAREILLY

The first challenge I faced in my circle was to solve a spate of road robberies that had terrorized the entire district. Three or four armed men would select a strategic point on an important road. Between 11 p.m. and 3 a.m., they would block the road with a bullock cart, empty drums, etc., at the selected point. As soon as a car would stop, they would loot it at gunpoint in the darkness. In order to prevent such crimes, the district police arranged for vehicles to travel in a convoy escorted by the police on all important roads during the night. But this required the involvement of too many police personnel. Hence, this practice started creating a problem.

My experiences in Agra had made me realize that perhaps the most efficient way to nab such robbers was to take them by surprise. So we devised a plan to ambush them. A sub-inspector and two constables were made to hide inside a decoy truck going towards Shahjahanpur from Faridpur late at night. They had hardly travelled 15–20 km when they saw an obstruction ahead. The truck driver stopped near the obstruction, as did another car. One of the armed robbers held up the car and forcibly pulled the gold bangles off the wrists of a woman passenger. The sub-inspector and constables started shooting at the robbers and two fell. The other two escaped. We used the same strategy again on a different stretch of road and again managed to bring down one robber. My out-of-the-box idea had worked, and I was exhilarated. Little did I know that much more was in store. The most dramatic case of my life awaited, a case involving a soldier, his broken heart and his revenge.

THE SAGA OF OMKAR SINGH YADAV

Omkar Singh Yadav was a sepoy of the Indian Army, posted in the northeast. On a visit home, he got married. Even though he had just spent a few days with his bride, he fell madly in love with her. He returned to his unit soon with a heavy heart, already looking forward to his next leave. But when he returned after a few months, he received a rude shock. His wife's own father had reportedly sold her to Shakti Singh, a man of ill repute in Dataganj in Badaun district, for a handsome amount! Omkar questioned his father-in-law, who insisted that Shakti Singh had taken the hapless girl away at gunpoint. Crazy with rage and anguish, Omkar shot his parents-in-law dead and left with his smoking gun for Dataganj. There, he first shot Shakti Singh dead. Then he went into hiding, his bloodlust still not satisfied. At Shakti Singh's funeral, Omkar shot two more of Shakti Singh's relatives, causing a stampede at the cremation ghat. He managed to escape in the melee.

The police, unable to trace him, was at their wits' end. The press was baying for Omkar's blood. In desperation, they went to Omkar's house and failing to unearth anything new, manhandled his old parents and damaged his house.

A few days passed in silence. One night, in a remote police outpost in Bareilly, an SI was sleeping on a cot in the open. The outpost had neither a boundary wall, nor a sentry on guard. The SI awoke to discover a gun on his chest. It was being cocked by Omkar Singh, who was on his horseback.

'What do you want?' the SI managed to stammer.

Omkar Singh said that if he or any other police officer ever went to his house and threatened his parents ever again, he'd kill him. Then he left, leaving the petrified SI to report the event to his superiors. The next day, the sensational news, reported widely in local newspapers, became a major source of embarrassment for the Bareilly Police.

The SSP was especially very upset and ordered a manhunt for Omkar, the like of which had never been done before. Omkar was constantly on the move to avoid being detected. Finally, tired of it all, he wrote to the SSP of Bareilly. He said that the police had been harassing him and his old parents, which had made him take this step. He signed off with a strangely poetic sentence: *'Tumhare dil mein nyay nahi, mere dil mein daya nahi.'* (You don't have justice in your heart, I don't have mercy in mine.)

The SSP called on me to lead 'Operation Omkar Singh' and ordered all police stations and circle officers in the district to extend me their full cooperation. This was an immense responsibility, one that both exhilarated and worried me. Once again, like the dacoits I'd chased in Agra, I was faced with a shadowy adversary who knew the lay of the land better than I did and had the sympathy of the locals. Again, it was time for some creative thinking.

Biting the Bullet

In a meeting with villagers in Faridpur, I offered handsome rewards for any actionable information we received on Omkar's whereabouts. In addition to five thousand rupees, a huge sum of money in those days, I also offered them a gun, firearm license and personal security if necessary. Two or three days later, I was in Faridpur to investigate a murder. On the way back, my car was flagged down by two villagers. They informed me that only half an hour ago, they had seen Omkar Singh on horseback, about four kilometres from Faridpur.

If we left immediately, we could probably catch him. But I had only three policemen with me, and the sun would set in another one-and-a-half hours. There seemed little chance of making contact with him. But I decided to go ahead anyway. I asked the two villagers to jump into my jeep and show us the way. Ahead of Faridpur, the informants led us down an unpaved road flanked by fields of tall sugarcane on either side. Beyond a scattering of huts lay the Hanuman temple where they said they had spotted Omkar.

There was still some time for the sun to set. We drove on, on what seemed like a wild goose chase. But then, a kilometre ahead, we spotted a figure on horseback along the sugarcane field. As we neared him, Omkar spotted us. I ordered him to surrender. Instead, he started firing at us. Ensuring a prudent distance, we gave chase. I took a shot in his direction, and the bullet hit his horse. Omkar fell down with the poor animal and disappeared into the sugarcane thickets. It was dark by then. Our search of the fields was fruitless. But as the SSP later pointed out, this was the first taste of the police's wrath that Omkar had received. The two informants were duly rewarded with the SSP's blessings. A few restless days passed, but we didn't get a break in the case.

One weekend, the DIG of Bareilly Range invited all the senior police officers in the city to lunch at his residence. While my wife and I were at the party, a man came to my house, saying he had important information for me. My sentry directed him to the DIG's house. When I eventually met him, he said he had left Omkar Singh lying on a cot inside an isolated hut in a village. Apparently, Omkar was not well and had asked my informant to fetch medicines and cartridges from the city.

It was afternoon. We had to cross two small rivers on bullock carts to reach our destination. Time was of essence. I left my wife at the party after being assured that she would be taken home safely. At Faridpur, the Inspector, along with all the available force, was already waiting. After crossing the first river in bullock carts, we hiked for about a kilometre to the second river. Then we finally reached the hut where Omkar was hiding.

It was a lonely spot. The mud and brick hut was tiny but had two points of entry. We surrounded it on all sides, and I called out his name.

'Omkar Singh, you are surrounded from all sides. It will be in your interest to surrender. You will be produced before the court of law, and you will get a chance to defend yourself.'

An anxious voice came from inside, 'Sahib, I am not

Biting the Bullet

Omkar Singh. There has been a mistake. You are arresting the wrong person. I am scared for my life. If I surrender, you will shoot me, mistaking me for the notorious gangster Omkar Singh. If I do not surrender, even then I'll meet the same fate...'

What if we had actually made a mistake? We had no photographs of Omkar Singh. Then I remembered something. When Omkar Singh had fired at me, I'd noticed he kept his revolver under his *kurta*. So I asked Head Constable Roop Singh to address the fugitive again and ask him to prove his identity.

The man replied, 'I am not Omkar Singh and please stop harassing an innocent person who is not well.' On my instructions, Roop Singh ordered him to take off his *kurta*. The fugitive had no option but to comply, and sure enough, there was a revolver hanging at his waist from a strap that hung over his shoulder, which Roop Singh reported to me.

'I now have no doubt that you are Omkar Singh,' I shouted. 'Surrender or else!'

Omkar Singh got to his feet, realizing his time was up. He surrendered his weapons one by one and then emerged from the hut with no further ado.

'I have surrendered to you, Sahib. Please tell me which way I should face, so that you can shoot me in a fake encounter.' he asked me.

I told him that we had no intention of shooting him but wanted to see him brought to the book for the many murders he had committed.

'You will be sent to jail and given a chance to stand trial

before a court of law. You will get a fair chance to defend yourself,' I said. But Omkar just could not bring himself to believe me. I realized that the man, like many in society, had lost trust in the system.

We took him into custody, and he requested for a cigarette. I asked one of the policemen to give him one. He then asked me to permit him to narrate his story before me. Once permitted, he narrated his unfortunate story. I realized that except the people he had killed to avenge the selling of his wife, neither had Omkar actually killed anyone else nor had he committed any other form of crime. I found myself pitying the man and what life had forced him to become. All I could suggest to him was to put up an impassioned defence and believe in the justice of god.

The next day, a huge crowd had gathered to see him when he was being produced before a magistrate. It felt as if the story of a man wronged by life had caught everyone's attention and sympathy. Eventually of course, he was sent to jail, but before leaving, he actually thanked me for sparing his life!

After his arrest, Omkar's old parents once again faced the wrath of some of the families of his victims. His house was also attacked and damaged. Omkar reported the matter to me from jail. When I had the matter investigated and found it to be true, I issued orders to ensure the safety of his parents. The local police were asked to look after them.

Over the years, Omkar wrote letters to me from jail, mostly to request me to help his old parents. I continued to help them from wherever I was posted. After several years and many transfers, I was posted back to Bareilly as the IG of Bareilly Zone. One day, when I was attending a public function chaired by a senior politician, I noticed the bodyguard standing behind him. He had a thick, silver moustache and wore a big turban. His eyes were more or less focused on me sitting in the front row, and he was gently smiling.

Once the function got over, he walked towards me with folded hands. He touched my feet and said, 'In the absence of any evidence against me, the court acquitted me in all the cases. However, I still had to spend about ten years in jail. I married again and I now have a family. All thanks to you, Sahib.'

He was Omkar Singh Yadav.

3
THE DACOITS OF AGRA

My posting to Bareilly proved to be lucky for me, not only professionally but personally too. My son—my first-born—came into our lives here, making me the happiest man alive. I still remember holding my newborn for the first time. The hands that had nabbed criminals, held pistols and fired rifles were shaking with nervous excitement as I held the baby. For the time being, I wanted to forget everything and just submerge myself in my happy world.

However, an image continued to haunt me. It was of the bullet-ridden body of the brave police officer Mahavir Singh, who had been mercilessly killed by Phoola and his paramour Gullo. I could not forget the helpless anger I had experienced when I realized I could do nothing at that time to bring his killer to justice.

It was time for the 1966 batch of IPS officers to be

promoted to superintendent of police (SP). All of us hoped to become the SP of a district, but destiny had slightly different plans for me. I was appointed SP all right, but not in charge of a district but of Anti-Dacoity Operations in Agra. I had been waiting for this day when I could go back to Agra and that day had come. The familiar but challenging terrain of the Chambal beckoned me, and I was enthused at the idea of getting a second chance to nab Phoola and Gullo.

I reached Agra and joined my new post. Since this was a recently created post, I had no designated office and very limited staff. By now, these were minor infrastructural issues that I was well used to dealing with. Other than me, there was one more SP dedicated to this job. We had one inspector each assigned to us, minimal clerical hands and a tented office in the Circuit House campus. Even the rudimentary stationary items were not available. I still remember using stones instead of paperweights here! Eventually, we were allotted an outhouse in the Circuit House and were able to get on with the task at hand.

CHASING DACOITS ON THEIR HOME GROUND

First, we listed all the dacoits operating in the Chambal ravines, some in UP and others in MP. These included Mohar Singh, Madho Singh and Phoola. All of them had rewards on their heads. Their gang members ranged from sixty to eighty, all armed with sophisticated semi-automatic weapons, sniper rifles and even close quarter battle (CQB) weapons. They moved from one location to another, usually during the day and preferred to rest at night. Contrary to what Bollywood movies portray, they never moved on horseback. Instead, they travelled on foot for long stretches at a time, which is the only practical way to move in the ravines. Their unparalleled knowledge of the ravines and immense stamina gave them a huge advantage over the police.

From the police's point of view, the most important gang was Phoola's. As for me, I had long dreamed of putting an end to this gang's reign of terror. By now, many members of Phoola's gang had become legends in their own right—Kunwarji Gadaria, Lajja Ram Pandit, Lal Singh, alias Laiyyan, and his paramour Gullo. All of them carried handsome rewards for their arrests.

The main question was how we should get started. All of us were new to our posts and had no contacts amongst the public. Like earlier, we had neither knowledge of the terrain, nor the local's ability to withstand the grievous summer heat of the Chambal ravines. For quite some time, these issues consumed our time. Narain Singh, the inspector attached to me, had been posted in Agra earlier and still had a few contacts there. I asked him to accompany me to the neighbouring sub-division of Dholpur, an area frequented by dacoit gangs. In those days, Dholpur was not a district as it is today. It used to be a sub-division of Bharatpur district. We met the additional superintendent of police (Addl. SP) of Dholpur at his office. He was able to give us some information regarding the Phoola gang and extended us all cooperation in our mission. Informal conversations with villagers along the way helped me realize one thing—if we were to be successful in nabbing these wily dacoits, we had to develop a good network of sincere and intelligent informers, locally known as *Mukhbirs*.

Mukhbirs have existed in the Chambal region for as long as the dacoits have flourished here. They are slippery customers, not at all easy to handle. Get hoodwinked by them, and one is likely to get badly double-crossed. But if a police officer who is an outsider doesn't trust his *Mukhbir*, he won't be able to do much in this area anyway. Striking the right balance is an art and getting the right *Mukhbir* is like hitting the jackpot.

Meanwhile, as we hunted for *Mukhbirs*, I decided to set up a crack unit to hunt down Phoola's gang. Each member of this unit would have to be physically very fit, under forty years of age and able to walk for miles in the summer heat to track the gang. They would also have to be very good marksmen and full of determination and confidence. We decided to choose members for this unit from the existing eight companies of the 15th Battalion of the PAC located in Agra. It was to be commanded and led by a young and able company commander from the same battalion and located at Iradat Nagar police station, which is on the border of Rajasthan. While we looked for information and informers, the unit exercised vigourously every morning and spent their days getting briefed on Phoola and his gang members and collected whatever intelligence they could.

Finally, we had our first lead. A man named Pooran from a village in Rajasthan came to meet me. First, he cautioned me against the *Mukhbirs* from his tribe. He averred that they were a slimy, untrustworthy lot who would praise an officer to the skies one minute, and double-cross him the next. I asked him what he does for a living. He said he was a farmer, but every now and again, he also gave information to the police. Should he give me accurate and actionable information, I asked, what sort of reward did he expect?

He asked for a double barrel 12-bore gun and half of the declared reward money. I agreed to his demand but told him that he would have to obtain the license for the gun himself. I also told him that if he tried to double-cross us, he'd be in serious trouble.

Later, I asked Narain Singh to find out more about Pooran. It turned out that he did possess some land, but it wasn't enough to sustain him. He liked his alcohol and was likely to be found in the village tavern in the evening. Soon, Pooran became a useful resource; he had good contacts and always had his ears and eyes open. Moreover, people tended to underestimate him as they thought he was just an insignificant alcoholic. In short, he was the perfect fly on the wall, the kind I desperately needed.

One day, I visited the crack unit (which I had named the Z Company) at the Iradat Nagar police station with Head Constable Ram Singh, who was to provide protection to me wherever I went. On our way back, we decided to return via Dholpur area, along with Ram Singh and Ravinder Singh, company commander of the Z Company. That was where we spotted Pooran near a bus stop. He said he was waiting to board a bus to Agra. He had information for me, but not about the Phoola gang.

'There is a one-man gang I wanted to give you some key information about,' he said.

THE LONE RANGER

Pooran was talking about the oldest living dacoit in the Chambal region—Ramdeen. Ramdeen was linked with the legendary gang of Man Singh but preferred to operate alone, with only his trusty 30 Springfield rifle (popularly known in the dacoit country as a *Pach Fera*). He was known to kidnap victims for ransom and had a big reward on his head. According to Pooran, Ramdeen was, at that very moment, sheltering in a nearby village. Apparently, he was not well and was alone. He had asked Pooran to get medicines for him. Instead, Pooran decided to inform me about the old dacoit.

We did not have any reinforcements, I said. Ramdeen could escape easily. Pooran said that we did not need heavy reinforcements to nab a sick old man. He said he was in a room with one door and a barred window. I was more cautious in my approach. Since we were only three police personnel, setting up a strong cordon round his room was impossible. I sent a wireless to the local police, requesting for additional force. Meanwhile, we recced the room and the area around it from a distance. It had a brownish door, and I wondered if we could simply lock Ramdeen inside the room. But what if he started firing at us?

Both Ram Singh and Ravinder Singh voiced their doubts about the plan, suggesting we wait for backup. Neither wanted to risk their lives just to catch one dacoit. But the sun was soon going to set. Our window of opportunity was shrinking. So I decided to lock Ramdeen's door myself. With Ram Singh to cover me from the right and Ravinder Singh from the left, I started the agonizingly slow crawl towards Ramdeen's door. In case he fired at me, they were supposed to fire at the window—the only place from where Ramdeen could shoot me. As soon as I reached the door, I jumped up and latched it. I had taken a big risk, but it was a cool and calculated one.

Sensing some noise, Ramdeen peered out of the window and shouted, *'Kaun hai, kaun hai?'* (Who is there? Who is there?) None of us replied. He settled down, and I slowly crawled back to safety. Now that Ramdeen was under our control, we wondered how to force him to surrender. In the meantime, one platoon (about thirty men) of Rajasthan Armed Constabulary (RAC) personnel led by the company commander, Lal Singh, arrived. Lal Singh was a controversial personality, known to have contacts with dacoits. Anyway, now that we had backup, I shouted to Ramdeen that we had locked him in and had him surrounded. If he surrendered, no harm would be done to him. Ramdeen started hurling abuses at the platoon, particularly singling out Lal Singh.

'Lal Sahib, tumne mujhe dhoka diya hai. Aur paisa chahiye tha toh mujhe bata dete. Tum bahaut baimaan ho.' (Lal Singh, you have betrayed me. If you wanted more money, you could have asked me. You are a cheat.) Lal Singh was embarrassed. He shouted back at Ramdeen.

'Tu bahaut ka****a hai. Tujhe hum jab chahte hum maar dete, par teri umar ka lihaaz kiya aur maara nahi, aur ab

tu humein galiyaa de raha hai?' (You are such a rascal. Had it not been for your age, we would have killed you long back. And now, you are abusing me?)

I simply had to intervene, and told Ramdeen that it was not Rajasthan Police but UP Police that had surrounded him. In the meanwhile, the tear gas squad also arrived from Agra. I called out to Ramdeen and told him that if he did not surrender immediately, we would have to gas him in the room. He replied, *'Mujhko policewalo par koi vishwas nahi hai aur police ke haat lagne se pahle mai khud ko goli maar loonga.'* (I don't trust the police. Before you people get hold of me, I will shoot myself.)

I asked the gas squad to fire a 100-yard shell at the door of the room. The shell hit the door with a loud bang, broke through it and exploded inside the room. The room was filled with gas. Ramdeen tried to cover his face with a bedsheet but that did not help him. Meanwhile, I had one more shell fired at the room. Ramdeen started choking, and he began to break. Ultimately, he agreed to surrender. I asked him to throw his rifle out of the window first. We finally took him into custody. The platoon was agog with excitement about the unconventional way in which I had forced Ramdeen to surrender.

Ramdeen was handed over to the Rajasthan Police and later sent to jail. He underwent trial and was convicted. When the DIG sent a report to the DGP about the arrest of Ramdeen and the unusual way in which it had been done, the DGP appreciated my efforts and sent me a special commendation for my achievement.

MY FIRST ENCOUNTER

The nabbing of Ramdeen helped me build relationships with several officers of the Rajasthan Police as well as with villagers. But somehow, information on Phoola continued to elude me. Even the Rajasthan Police, which included the Rajakhera and Dholpur police stations, had nothing to report about any movement by the Phoola gang. I called Pooran to ask him what was happening. How could it be possible that such a large gang could move around the region with impunity but leave no trace behind? In our experience, dacoit gangs liked to move from one location to another in the interest of safety. My sense was that even if people had some useful intelligence, they were unwilling to share it. If we couldn't reach the information, perhaps we had to find a way for the information to reach us...

Pooran reported that Phoola's gang had been active in some villages of Dholpur recently: 'I've heard that this gang has been visiting the village of Tor every now and then and has been seen mingling with the villagers there without hesitation.'

I asked Pooran to hang around in Tor, build contacts there and see if he could collect more information about the presence of the gang in the village. To save precious hours from our reaction time, I decided to work out of the nearby Iradat Nagar police station for the next few days. This way, he too could relay the information to me swiftly. I briefed the company commander of Z Company to get his team ready to leave at short notice for a long drawn out operation. Six days later, Pooran informed us that about half of Phoola's gang had been staying in Tor village for the past few days.

This was the moment we had all been preparing for! Pooran drew a plan of Tor, marking out a cluster of houses where the gang members were staying. This area was on higher ground compared to the rest of Tor. He also introduced us to Nanku, a resident of Tor. Nanku turned out to be Pooran's contact in the village and a valuable resource for us.

Both Pooran and Nanku advised that we should lay siege on Tor village immediately. But I assessed that a siege would require eight to ten companies of armed police. We had only one. Such an act seemed doomed to failure.

Instead, I decided to wait and prepare for the operation. The SSP of Agra was asked to provide us with at least six companies of PAC as soon as possible. Since Tor village was in Rajasthan, the support and co-operation of the Rajasthan Police was an absolute necessity. I decided to go to the residence of the Addl. SP of Dholpur to apprise him of the situation and request his help and cooperation. Time was of essence, I emphasized, as the gang was constantly on the move. We simply had to act immediately. The Addl. SP was excited to hear this as Phoola and his gang had been a thorn in their flesh for a long time. However, as per orders of the SP of Bharatpur, he could act only after getting his consent, but he was unfortunately in Jaipur. In those days of only landline phones, contacting people in a different town was not that easy a matter, as it is today. I was overcome by the urgency of the matter and told him that since the dacoits were not going to wait for us, I'd like to launch the operation as soon as possible. All he could do was to detail one company of RAC along with an experienced and capable officer in charge, Lakhu Singh, with us.

THE TOR OPERATION

It took us about one hour to reach Tor. Lakhu Singh met us there with the RAC Company. Between us, we had only two companies at our disposal, still not enough to lay a proper cordon around the village. Lakhu Singh and I decided to cordon off as large an area as possible. The gaps would be covered by the line of sight, at least while there was daylight. Towards the north of Tor was the railway line running between Agra and Mumbai. On the southern side was the Agra-Gwalior highway. It was decided that Lakhu Singh and the RAC company should surround the eastern side of the village. The Z Company would surround the western side. I advised Lakhu Singh that his company should avoid using the light machine guns (LMGs) to the extent possible. The idea was that if they attempted to escape by breaking the cordon, the LMGs could take them by surprise. We all wished each other good luck and god speed, and proceeded to our respective positions to lay the cordon.

We had barely started laying the western cordon when we saw people running on the railway tracks. I realized that the gang had already been alerted of our presence and were trying to escape even before the cordon was completed.

Biting the Bullet

The two in front had rifles with them and ran much faster than the group behind them. Our company was on full alert when one of the dacoits while running, fired two or three shots at us. I asked the Havaldar close to me to fire back. Coincidentally, he was carrying an LMG on his shoulder. Instead of taking position on the ground to fire the weapon (which is the usual way to fire an LMG), he quickly brought the LMG to his shoulder and fired a couple of bursts towards the fleeing bandits and hit both of them. Both fell to the ground.

We were able to then complete the cordon and were now in position to take care of any other bandits who would try to escape. Lakhu Singh called me on the wireless after hearing the shots that had been fired in the skirmish. I told him what had happened. However, there were still huge gaps in the cordons on the northern and southern sides. Hence, we could not afford to be aggressive and try to enter the village. Just then, Lady Luck smiled upon us. To my pleasant surprise, I found that three more PAC companies had arrived from Agra, under the command of a seasoned Assistant Commandant Jai Pal Singh. He was a very capable officer, who had served in the army earlier. I briefed him about the prevailing situation and asked him to send two companies to strengthen the cordons on the northern and southern sides of the village. We would hold one company in reserve. Thus, by sunset, we had surrounded the entire village.

Just then, we had a surprise visitor. It was none other than the legendary Shankar Singh, the SP of Bharatpur, along with a small police party. He came bearing dinner, which was very thoughtful as none of us had had any opportunity to eat a morsel. Shankar Singh had a singularly impressive personality. His was more than six feet tall and had a luxurious brown moustache that matched his brown eyes. In my estimation, he was the most highly decorated officer in the force at that time, having been awarded the Ashoka Chakra, Padma Shri and every other possible medal. Protocol demanded that I asked him to lead this operation.

I briefed him on everything that had transpired thus far. He said nothing could be done during the night. Instead, we should wait till daybreak and then attack the village from three sides. Just then, a volley of bullets came from the direction of the village and narrowly missed us! This infuriated Shankar Singh. He started shouting at the dacoits to come out and fight like men and not behave as cowards. He was standing, obliviously some bullets whizzed past every now and then. I advised him to take cover, else he could get shot. Typical of him, Shankar Singh retorted: 'A bullet to kill me is yet to be made!'

Meanwhile, someone from the village shouted back, saying that Shankar Singh had taken money from them for giving them shelter—why was he now siding with the UP Police? They were willing to give him more, they added. As I was dodging bullets and trying to figure out our next move, I began wondering if this supposed nexus between the dacoits and police was the reason why dacoits operated in Agra with such impunity. Or was this simply their wily tactic to divide our ranks? I didn't have a clue, but this was not the time to think about it.

Biting the Bullet

Suddenly, we saw a dust storm coming towards us. It was no ordinary dust storm; this had been created by the dozens of cattle, buffaloes, pigs, camels, etc., of the village that the gangsters had forced to stampede in our direction. Behind the animals, we could see the dacoits trying to escape. We had no choice but to open fire. Several animals fell, adding to the confusion. Seeing our bullets, the dacoits retreated to the village. Then, before we could get used to the lull, they would try to escape again. This went on for some more time. We were all exhausted but elated that our cordon had succeeded in hemming the dacoits in successfully.

Just before midnight, the SSP of Agra arrived at the scene. By now, we had a smaller cordon outside the main one, where the villagers, who had been caught trying to escape, were being interrogated. Amongst them was one who claimed to be the nephew of the notorious Kunwarji Gadaria. He had come to deliver food to his uncle, he said. Others were constantly being questioned too. Meanwhile, we fine-tuned our plan to storm the village from the east, west and south, leaving the northern side through which the Agra-Bombay railway line passed, open. The idea was to capture anyone trying to escape from there. We synchronized our watches and left for our designated posts.

6 a.m. was the Zero Hour.

THE ZERO HOUR

Soon after my men and I started for the village, firing resumed. We immediately took cover. One of my men was hit, but not critically. He was immediately sent to the hospital. I narrowly escaped being hit by one when Havaldar Moolchand, who had played football with me in the Agra district police football team, pushed me out of danger. He pointed towards a window on the second story of a building in front from where a sten gun had been pointing moments before. He fired at the window with his Thomson Machine Carbine (TMC) and we moved on. Every couple of yards, a dacoit would take potshots at us and then disappear. This deadly game of hide and seek continued till the team coming from the southern side opened fire with an LMG. Some gangsters ran towards the northern side. The police was waiting for them there too and opened fire with their LMGs. Three dacoits fell.

All of us managed to regroup finally in the centre of Tor. A quick count revealed that as many as thirteen members of the Phoola gang, including two of the main lieutenants of the gang, Kunwarji Gadaria and Lajja Ram Pandit, had been killed. This was a shattering blow to the gang and a major achievement for us. But it came at a huge cost. An innocent woman had also been killed in the crossfire. The carcasses of several animals lay on the ground. Two policemen had been wounded, one rather severely. The SP of Bharatpur immediately promised compensation to be paid by the state government to the affected persons.

The entire operation had lasted for almost nineteen hours. Exhausted, hungry and filthy, I finally reached my home and family. After a good meal, I fell into a deep sleep. The next morning, I found everyone, including my superiors, elated by the successful culmination of the operation. I was happy too, but all I could think was that Phoola had once again eluded me. While he roamed free, my mission could never be regarded as complete.

THE DEMISE OF THE PHOOLA GANG

With the deaths of Kunwarji Gadaria and Lajja Ram Pandit, the Phoola gang was crippled. Lal Singh, alias Laiya, and Gullo, his lover, became its backbone. Since Laiya belonged to a village in the jurisdiction of Nibhora police station of Agra district, I thought he would perhaps be easier to nab compared to other members of the gang, who were mostly from Rajasthan. It turned out that other than his widowed mother Anaar Devi, who lived alone in Salempur Dhangar village in the jurisdiction of Nibhora police station, Laiya had no other family. Perhaps Anaar Devi could be used as a means to reach Laiya.

The question was, who could help me get in touch with her? I thought of driving to her village incognito. My personal security men and I dressed in civilian clothes and set off. We reached her village and after leaving our vehicle at a distance, I, along with my security men, tried to familiarize ourselves with the village. Over the next few days, we visited Anaar Devi's village two or three times more, usually near sunset. Our focus was only her house and the area around it. Meanwhile, we were trying to get some leads on her.

Some days later, one of the constables who had

accompanied us to Salempur came to see me in my office. His name was Amar Singh. He told me that he had a relative in that village and might be able to arrange a meeting for me with Anaar Devi. I told him to do so but insisted that confidentiality was of the utmost importance. Amar Singh returned after two days and told me that Anaar Devi had agreed to meet me in my office. She arrived the next day, veiled from head to toe. Amar Singh was with her. I told her that I needed her help to save her only son. She told me her story.

Anaar Devi had been widowed when Laiya was barely five years old. Growing up without a father, the teenage boy fell into bad company. In spite of her being very harsh on him, he continued to enjoy staying in the company of anti-social elements. He was not fond of studying and eventually dropped out. When he was older, he joined the Phoola gang. At this point, her voice began to quiver. Soon, she was weeping inconsolably.

I asked if she would like her son to leave the gang and start living with her again. As she heard these words, she immediately sat up. How would that even be possible, she asked. I replied that if she could persuade Laiya to inform us about Phoola, he could get a chance to live life all over again. I would get him to surrender and then send him to jail. He would stand trial in all the cases he was wanted. Since there would hardly be any evidence against him, he would be acquitted and released from jail. He could then come home and start life afresh. But all this would happen, I reiterated, only if he turned into an informer.

Biting the Bullet

Anaar Devi was doubtful. Laiya was Phoola's most trusted confidant and would never betray him, she said. If she persuaded her son that this was his only chance to start all over again, I said, then perhaps he could agree. Otherwise, there was a strong chance that like Kunwarji Gadaria and Lajja Ram Pandit, Laiya, too could fall to a police bullet. Eventually, she said that she would do whatever it took to try and save her son.

We gained valuable intelligence about Laiya's movements from her. Apparently, he came to see her very often but always without warning. I told her that whenever he visited next, she should explain to him the offer I had just made to her. Initially, he would probably be angry, but she must be patient with him. I said that she should then try and convince him to meet me secretly at a place of their choice. I promised to come alone. I called Constable Amar Singh to the room and told her that he should keep in touch with her, and that if she ever wanted to send a message to me, she could do so through him.

People often imagine that there are thrills every minute in a policeman's job. The fact is that we spend much of our time simply waiting for things to happen. In this case, too, after this very satisfactory conversation with Anaar Devi, days passed with no news.

Then one day, we got the news that Phoola, who had been fuming about the encounter in Tor and had been angry with the Rajasthan Police as well as the people of Tor for their role in it, had murdered four people near the village. Apparently, he had declared that he won't even spare a dog belonging to Tor! This multiple murder sent shockwaves through Dholpur and Bharatpur. This was Phoola's first crime in Rajasthan; he had only operated in UP before this. The Inspector General (IG) of Rajasthan Police conveyed his great displeasure to Shankar Singh and mounted pressure on him, who was still the SP of Bharatpur.

Shankar Singh ordered a huge operation to mount pressure on Phoola and his gang. Anybody with even the slightest connection with Phoola or members of his gang was picked up for interrogation. He came to my DIG and requested him for my services. So the next day, I reached Dholpur.

Shankar Singh and I drove to the camp being conducted by the Dholpur Police under the supervision of the ASP of Dholpur. Dozens of people were being roughly interrogated here but no worthwhile information was forthcoming. Then, we received information that Phoola had visited the Pureni village in the Chambal ravines with some of his gang members. This village had become quite notorious, as it had previously harboured the Lakhan gang. The SP of Bharatpur immediately planned a big operation in the night. We walked for about two hours to reach the village. By 4 a.m., it was completely surrounded. Search parties were sent into the village at dawn. Unfortunately, we could not achieve any success. In the morning, the villagers offered milk and tea to us, which was very welcome, as it had been a very cold night and the morning was equally chilly. That was when we got to know that we were exactly one day late. Phoola had indeed stayed in the village one night earlier but had left in the morning. We were very disappointed, but such failures in the ravines were commonplace. The operation was called off. Exhausted and disappointed, I returned to Agra.

THE FIRST BREAK

The next few days proved fruitful. Amar Singh came to my office and informed me that Anaar Devi wanted to meet me. Laiya had come to visit her. He was furious when he heard his mother had been communicating with the police.

'Had I been anyone but his mother, I think Laiya would have killed me for saying such things!' she said. Anaar Devi advised her son to think about it when his temper had cooled down. 'At first, I had no hope, as he had left my house so furious with me,' she said. 'But to my surprise, he returned after only three days to talk to me again...' Apparently, Laiya had had a change of heart.

He asked his mother if she trusted me. When she replied in the affirmative, Laiya asked her to arrange a meeting with me. And now came the twist. Anaar Devi told me that only sometime back, Laiya had revealed to her that Gullo, Phoola's paramour, was now attracted to him. He suspected that in case Phoola came to know of this, he would kill them both. He wanted to leave the gang with Gullo, as that was the only way they could be together. Perhaps this was why he had agreed so quickly to meet me, I deduced. Anyway, that day when Anaar Devi left my office, I felt hopeful after a very long time that my efforts would finally bear fruit.

She returned in a week's time and confirmed that Laiya

would meet me after three days. 'He will meet you on the condition that you do not tell anyone else in the police about it. Also, you have to promise to come unarmed and alone,' she said. I agreed. The meeting would take place at 9 p.m. at Anaar Devi's house. I cautioned Anaar Devi to also maintain the strictest secrecy, as it was the only way to ensure her son's safety.

THE MEETING WITH LAIYA AND GULLO

Finally, the day dawned when I would get to see what Laiya, the man I had been tracking for so many days, was all about! I left for Anaar Devi's house in Salempur Dhangar village in a civilian vehicle, wearing plain clothes. Although I had agreed to come alone and unarmed, with me were four handpicked men, two head constables and two constables, also in plain clothes. One of the selected constables was Amar Singh. All were armed with close-combat weapons.

The pre-monsoon weather was hot and humid. We stopped a hundred metres short of Anaar Devi's house. The house was dimly lit. I instructed three men to hide in the fields of Arhar, ensuring that they were within fifty yards from me and had the house in clear view. They were to stay hidden and come out from their positions only if they heard gunfire or suspected something was afoot. Amar Singh and I walked to Anaar Devi's residence, but only I went in.

A lantern was burning inside and the light was dim. I could see the figure of Anaar Devi and two other figures of

Biting the Bullet

a well-built man and a slim tall woman, standing with their backs to me. They turned and I realized, with a thrill, that I was at last face-to-face with Laiya and Gullo! It felt strange, surreal even, to see the two notorious gangsters, carrying such big rewards for their arrests, right in front of me.

Time was of essence, so I immediately came to the point. If Laiya chose to help me bring Phoola and his entire gang to justice, I would ensure that he would be fairly treated in jail and after serving his time, start his life afresh. Laiya said he was ready to help me, but on one condition. I must do the same for Gullo so that she, too, could reclaim her life as a free woman. I agreed.

The key question was, how would he inform me? It would be futile to have too much of a time lag between his passing on the information to me and my being able to act upon it. Laiya said that he could give information to his mother and she could relay it to me. This could prove difficult. The lady had no access to a phone. In the pre-mobile phone era, communication was a real challenge. I told Anaar Devi that I would think of a way out. The meeting ended, and I could see a cautious optimism in the eyes of Laiya and Gullo.

In the next few days, I spent much of my time thinking about the quickest way for Anaar Devi to send me information. Only one solution came to mind, which was to station Amar Singh somewhere close to Salempur Dhangar village. He would meet Anaar Devi once at least in two days at different locations for updates. The system worked.

One day, Laiya informed me that Phoola, along with some of his gang members, was planning on attending a marriage in a nearby village. We made all the preparations for an ambush, only to learn that he changed his plans at the last minute.

A BOLT FROM THE BLUE

I was completely engrossed in this cat and mouse game with Phoola when I was hit by a bolt from the blue. My transfer orders had been issued! I was asked to take over immediately as SP of Mainpuri. I did not want a transfer at this stage, not when I was so close to nabbing Phoola and his gang. I requested my DIG to get my transfer cancelled. Although the posting was prestigious and advantageous to my career, I said that bringing Phoola to justice had become a personal ambition for me. The DIG finally agreed to forward my application to the DGP with the recommendation that my request be sanctioned.

While I was waiting for the result of my petition, the then government of UP fell, and in its place, a Congress government was installed. My earlier posting as the SP of Mainpuri was cancelled; instead, I was posted as ASP Banaras! I just could not understand the logic of this.

I was worried about Laiya and Gullo's fate. My meeting with them and the understanding that we had reached could cost them their lives. I had to do something for them before I left Agra. I thought the best way to safeguard them was to arrest them. If they were not convicted in the cases against them, they would be released from jail and would get a chance to start life again. That way, they would be safe not only from Phoola but also from unscrupulous policemen who might be tempted to bump them off for the reward they were carrying on their heads. I gave information about the whereabouts of Laiya and Gullo to the inspector of Rakabganj police station, with whom I had a good understanding. I also requested him to include the constables, who had worked tirelessly with me on the case in the arrest party, so that they could at least get a share of the reward that was indeed their due. In two days, both Laiya and Gullo were in jail.

As for me, duty dictated that I obey orders given to me by my superiors. So I left Agra for Banaras with a very heavy heart and a lingering sense of unfinished business. The thought that I could not liquidate Phoola hurt me very much. I derived some solace from the fact that I had virtually destroyed his gang; even Laiya and Gullo were in jail now. It was only a matter of time before Phoola would ultimately meet his end. However, I would not have the satisfaction of witnessing it...

4

BANARAS: A TRICKY TERRAIN

The story goes that Mirza Asadullah Baig Khan, popularly known as Ghalib, was passing through Banaras en route to Calcutta (now Kolkata). He was so mesmerized by Banaras city that he ended up staying there for two months. Like Ghalib's, my tryst with Banaras was supposed to be short, but I ended up staying there for over one year! Here's what happened.

When the Congress government suddenly assumed power in UP, Kamalapati Tripathi became the new CM. Tripathi belonged to Banaras; he was an old freedom fighter and the city's most illustrious son at that time. Banaras was also his political constituency. Most of all, he was a *pucca* Banarasi—non-pretentious, self-assured and down to earth—who was in love with his hometown. As soon as he took charge as the CM, Banaras district suddenly assumed a greater significance, not only politically but also administratively. The bureaucracy of the district was changed, and it is said that the CM himself cherry-picked all top officials posted there. I happened to be one of them.

It is said that *'Lucknow ki shaam aur Banaras ki subah mashoor hain'* (the evenings in Lucknow and the mornings in Banaras are famous). Perhaps it was the sight of mellow dawn breaking over the city's ancient ghats or the light of a thousand lamps brightening the Ganges at dusk that inspired Ghalib to label Banaras as *Kaba-e-Hindustan*, or the Mecca of India. But administratively, few cities are as complicated as Banaras. Professional *goonda*s, communal factions, a fractious student community and politicians of all hues make the city a seething cauldron ready to spill over at the slightest pretext.

I joined my duties at the same time as the newly appointed district magistrate (DM) and the SSP, both very competent officers. Unfortunately, the wife of the SSP was taken quite ill in the intense summer heat and needed to recuperate in a cooler place. So the SSP had to go on leave, leaving me in charge. With no experience of administering a district and that too, a complicated one like Banaras, I was understandably nervous at the prospect. My first challenge came sooner than I had anticipated.

QUELLING MY FIRST COMMUNAL RIOT

Within days of my taking charge, a contentious bill was introduced in the Lok Sabha. Although it pertained to Aligarh Muslim University (AMU), which is almost 700 km away from Banaras, its repercussions were felt rather strongly here. Established by Sir Syed Ahmad Khan in 1875, AMU had the status of being a minority institution. The Muslim community was very sensitive to the autonomy this institution enjoyed and did not want any infringement in this respect. Hence, when the Aligarh Muslim University Amendment Bill was introduced in the Lok Sabha, they were not pleased.

The Muslim community in Banaras decided to gather force and launch a large-scale protest against the Bill on a Friday. The DM went away for a site inspection for a new hundred-bed hospital that the CM wanted to inaugurate. I had requested him to postpone his visit to another date in view of the very sensitive communal situation in the city. He turned down my request telling me that the city magistrate will all the time be available with me.

I had to handle the situation alone. Early next morning, just as we had finished checking all the security arrangements in the city, we were informed that a huge crowd had collected near Langde Hafiz Ki Masjid, which fell in the jurisdiction of Dashashwamedh police station. All it took was a couple of incendiary speeches and the crowd became restive. Some people had started throwing bricks. By the time we reached the scene, there was a crowd of about three thousand people, shouting slogans and pelting stones. A PAC picket posted for duty at this spot had already been overrun and most of its men had been injured and could hardly stand on their feet. When they saw me approach with just four policemen, they advised me to retreat and take shelter far away from the mob till more force arrived. I asked for the tear gas squad, which was located nearby. I also instructed for an additional company of PAC to be dispatched as soon as possible to the spot.

Meanwhile, I tried to engage the leader of the mob by speaking to him on a loud hailer. I tried to tell him that since Section 144 had been enforced, the gathering was illegal, and that they must disperse immediately. If they did not follow instructions, the police would have no other option but to disperse the crowd by force. Overtaken by mob frenzy, the leader was very abusive in his reply. A big stone was hurled in my direction. It shattered the windscreen of my jeep. More stones followed and then, some makeshift incendiary devices. Fortunately, none of us was injured.

Once the tear gas squad had arrived, I gave the mob one last warning on the loud hailer. Since the mob continued to pelt stones, I asked for a tear gas gun with a hundred-yard shell. I fired a shell in the direction of the leader of the mob. It exploded loudly near him and injured him in the thigh. The members of the mob began to shout: '*Firing ho gai, firing ho gai*' (they have started firing at us), and began to run helter-skelter. The mob had been dispersed without a lathi charge or resorting to fire. Meanwhile, the PAC company I had asked for had also arrived. They immediately took charge and arrested dozens of miscreants. The person who had been injured was sent to a hospital.

A serious situation had been deferred, not averted. There was a strong possibility that the mob would be incited into violence after the traditional Jumma ki Namaz (Friday prayers) that afternoon. It was imperative to impose a precautionary curfew. However, the DM felt that the CM would not take kindly to his constituency and hometown being placed under curfew. How could we think of bringing the entire city to a standstill, he asked. Eventually, the political perspective prevailed.

As soon as the Friday prayers were over, the city was engulfed by violence, and the police had to resort to firing at nearly thirteen different locations. The result of these firings was that the violence stopped for the time being, but anger simmered amongst the Muslims.

The incidents in Banaras sent shockwaves to Lucknow and Delhi. The Additional Inspector General of Police, the second in seniority in state police, was asked to reach Banaras and camp there for some time. He reached Banaras late in the night. The city was still resounding with battle cries of *'Allah-o Akbar'* and *'Har Har Mahadev'*. Several incidences of brickbatting were reported during the night. Most of these were directed at police pickets in alleys too narrow for vehicles to pass through. Many policemen were injured. I myself had stones pelted at me but got away with a minor injury.

THE AFTERMATH OF THE RIOT

The CM arrived to review the situation in Banaras in the aftermath of the violence. He took a round of the city and met many people throughout the day. The next morning,

Biting the Bullet

he summoned the DM and me to his residence. He was sitting on the floor getting his beard shaved by a barber when we entered his room. We also sat on the ground and gave him a complete report of all that had happened. While he was talking to us, he received a call from Indira Gandhi, the then prime minister. We could not hear what the prime minster had to say but could tell from the CM's responses that she was not happy with the way the situation had been handled. She felt that excessive action had been taken against the minority community. Some people from the minority community had personal contact with her. They felt that the police was prejudiced in taking action against Muslims and had used more force against them as compared to the Hindus. However, when she asked the CM to suspend both the DM and the SSP, he defended us staunchly. He told her that he had seen things for himself and had spoken to a lot of residents of Banaras. There had been no lapses in administration, he said. In fact, owing to the efficient handling of the riot, a difficult situation had been controlled well in time.

His support saved us from being suspended but could not prevent a high-level enquiry being ordered against us. The enquiry committee, headed by the home secretary of the government of UP found us not guilty. Another committee was then set up to make further enquires. This enquiry continued for about two to three years, but fortunately, it also failed to find any administrative lapses committed by us.

Ajai Raj Sharma

THE LULL AFTER THE STORM

After this stormy period was over, life slowly started to normalize. However, it took some time for me to appreciate the city that Ghalib and indeed, legions of travellers before and after him, had waxed eloquent about. It took a while for me to walk through its picturesque alleys and bylanes without remembering hapless policemen bloodied by brickbats for simply doing their jobs.

Eventually, however, the city's magic began to envelop me. Some of the most famous musicians of the country like tabla maestros Kishan Maharaj and Gudai Maharaj, vocalist Girija Devi and the internationally known shehnai player Bismillah Khan were from Banaras and performed regularly. I found it interesting that often, these concerts were attended by people from all walks of life—boatmen, rickshaw pullers, industrialists and aristocrats, all loved the music that was such an intrinsic part of the culture of Banaras. I also resumed playing tennis at the Banaras Club, where sometimes I would play with Kashi Naresh, the erstwhile Raja of Varanasi, who was not only a keen tennis player, but a very good one too.

Just as I was beginning to settle down, the ground beneath my feet began to shift once again. The state minister for home at that time was Radha Krishan Goswamy. He hailed from Banda district, which used to be one of the most backward and crime-prone districts of the state. Being the head of the home department in the state, he was always being pulled up in the state assembly for serious cases of crime taking place in Banda. He was, therefore, looking for an appropriate officer who could control the increasing crime in Banda. His eyes fell on me, and he started lobbying for me to be posted as the SP of Banda.

From what I had heard, Banaras was a cakewalk compared to Banda! Most of the MLAs in the district belonged to the Communist Party, who were always opposing the administration and clashing with the police. The local press was mostly yellow press, perpetually writing against government officials and blackmailing those at the junior levels. As for the criminals of Banda—the less said, the better! All the senior officers posted in Banaras advised me to appeal to the CM to post me to a more 'decent' place. It was almost discouraging.

Then, an inspector made me see my posting in a different light. Inspector Pandey, the Inspector of Banaras Kotwali, was one of those bold officers with a reputation of being very tough on criminals. He had been posted in Banda for quite some time before coming to Banaras. He congratulated me on my posting and said that I was ideally suited for the job. My out-of-the box approach to maintaining law and order was bound to be successful in Banda, he averred. He was the first person to encourage me to take on the challenge, and I decided to proceed to Banda.

In hindsight, I wish I had told him then how much his encouragement had meant to me. But before I could meet him again, he had been killed in an encounter with dacoits in Etah district.

5

BANDA: THE WILD WEST

Rishwat (bribe), *Bombard* (bombing), *Machis* (matchbox), *Kaichi* (a pair of scissors)—would you believe that these were the names of local newspapers in Banda when I reached there? The yellow press of Banda at that time used to run hair-raising headlines that would have been amusing if they had not been so irresponsible. The first article I saw there was about my predecessor leaving Banda and it was entitled: '*Banda ka ek aur phora phoota*' (Another boil of Banda has burst).

Each of these newspapers had a distinct editorial line. *Rishwat* focused on news of government officials who took bribes and indulged in corruption, while *Bombard*, *Kaichi* and *Machis* dealt with crimes in the district and the high-handed behaviour of government officials, especially police personnel. Soon after I settled down in Banda, I realized that these publications actually reflected the sad state of affairs in the district. There was a complete mistrust of government machinery, scant regard for police and administration and frustration all around. Inhospitable terrain, barren land and virtually no employment opportunities had turned Banda into a district of despair.

Banda district was huge but it was a prisoner of its geography. Nestled on the border of Uttar Pradesh and Madhya Pradesh, this district in Bundelkhand produced only two things in abundance—tendu leaves (used to make *bidi*s) and illegal firearms. One of its sub-divisions had a vast forest cover with wild animals, including panthers and tigers, abound.

THE GUN CULTURE OF BANDA

Men in Banda were very fond of firearms. It was said that what jewellery was to women, guns were to the men of Banda. People who had influence or money used to keep licensed weapons. Those who couldn't get a license found it incredibly easy to obtain an illegal firearm from the large number of illicit firearm manufactories there. I am reminded of a president of a students' union of a degree college in Banda who possessed a firearm license and used to carry his rifle to his class. On entering the classroom, he would go and place his rifle in one corner and sit down in his seat. Incredibly, his behaviour, that too in an educational institution, did not cause anyone to bat an eyelid!

Perhaps this fondness for firearms and their easy availability were among the reasons why there were so many murders in Banda. In fact, I observed that murders in Banda inevitably followed a cyclical pattern. Whenever someone was murdered, his family would definitely, at some time or the other, retaliate and take revenge by murdering a member of their opponent's family. Hence, once a murder was committed it sowed the seed for another murder by way of revenge. This evil cycle would go on. I hope that by this time, such obnoxious traditions have disappeared.

After I took over as the SP of Banda, a shocking incident took place. One day, during the final intermediate examination, a student was caught cheating. When the teacher intervened, the student took out a knife, stabbed him to death and managed to escape. Of course, there was a big hue and cry. It turned out that the accused was the son of a class three revenue official in Banda. Immediately, rumours began circulating that the police were in cahoots with the accused, that they would not catch him but instead actually help him evade the law.

The incident had taken place around 9 a.m. By 5 p.m., the accused still hadn't been traced. Meanwhile, anger against the police was running high and the public was up in arms.

How could I break that level of mistrust between the public and the police? I decided to call for a public meeting the next evening and invited politicians, members of the press, public persons and policemen to it. In the meanwhile, we had managed to catch the accused but kept it a secret. I asked members of the public to speak first. All of them criticized the police on various counts. None had anything to say in favour of the police. The press fraternity also stood up and lambasted the police. An MLA got up and remarked that this meeting was probably giving the new SP (that was me), a fair idea of what people thought about the police.

After hearing all of them, I got up and humbly accepted all their complaints and said I'd try and improve the existing situation. However, I said, as citizens they too had their duties. They must report crime. If they witness a crime, they must come forward to give their testimony. Then, I asked them what punishment they thought would be fitting for the student who stabbed his invigilator. They replied that he should be shot dead.

A collective gasp went up when we suddenly brought the accused boy out. I asked an inspector to tie his hands and feet and make him stand against a wall. The members of the public were horrified. They begged me not to kill the boy in their presence. I made them aware of their double standards in demanding that the police give extreme punishment to criminals, but they themselves would look the other way. The meeting ended with the consensus being that the new SP meant business.

A STATE OF *GOONDA* RAJ

To get Banda's affairs in order, I had to first deal with all the *goonda*s who had held the town to ransom all this time. Two *goonda*s were most feared—Mahendra Singh and Lalta Singh. Both had committed numerous crimes, but their victims and witnesses alike were too scared to report cases against them. Consequently, the police could also not do much. In the few cases that had been registered against them, both of them would waltz in and out of jail, surrendering at will and being instantly bailed out.

The inspector of the Banda police station was Akbar Singh, a tough officer with the reputation of being rough in his dealings with ordinary people. When I told him I proposed to take action against Mahendra Singh and Lalta Singh, he was taken aback. He said it would probably result in nothing but my transfer, as the two were very well connected and highly influential.

A few days later, a hostel student of a local college lodged a complaint with the police that Mahendra Singh had robbed him of the entire money he had received from home for his fees and monthly expenses. He named Mahendra Singh in the FIR. Akbar Singh decided to use this opportunity to arrest the *goonda*. But this wouldn't be easy: Mahendra Singh came from a well-connected family. His father, being an advocate, was a member of the Bar Association and was an office bearer of the Congress Party.

I advised Akbar Singh to get a platoon of PAC to surround Mahendra Singh's house, before trying to enter. I also told him to take Mahendra Singh by surprise by starting the action at 4 a.m. That's what he did. Instead of Mahendra, his father Dharmendra Singh opened the door. He said he would not allow the police to take his son without a warrant. Akbar Singh argued that a case of robbery had been registered against him and hence a warrant was not required. The father replied that in the absence of a warrant, he would resort to firing in order to prevent the police from taking his son to the police station. Other family members joined to prevent Akbar Singh from arresting Mahendra. Eventually, with great difficulty but with minimal use of force, the police was able to take Mahendra into custody.

Dharmendra Singh incited all the advocates of Banda to go on an indefinite strike in protest. Locals were thrilled to see the *goonda*, who had terrorized them for so long, go to jail. When they learned that the advocates had gone on a strike against Banda police, they organized a movement against the advocates. The shopkeepers refused to sell goods to advocates and the rickshaw pullers refused to ferry an advocate in their rickshaws. This made news. Even the *BBC* covered it.

Not to be outdone, Dharmendra Singh used all his contacts in Lucknow to get Akbar Singh transferred out of Banda. I sent a wireless message to the IG, home secretary and my DIG in Jhansi, informing them about the incident. I mentioned that twenty-seven cases under the Indian Penal Code had been registered in the past against Mahendra Singh and that Akbar Singh had simply acted on my orders. In spite of my best efforts, Akbar Singh received his transfer orders that very evening.

The public was unsettled and I, in a quandary. If this was the prize honest officers could expect for doing their duty, law and order could never be controlled. I sent another urgent wireless message to Lucknow, saying that the transfer of Akbar Singh had demoralized the Banda Police and the public. If his transfer could not be stopped, I should also be transferred along with him as he had acted on my orders.

And if that was not possible, then I should be permitted to proceed on a long leave. Finally, Akbar Singh's orders were reversed.

THE SAGA OF LALTA SINGH

They say power is an aphrodisiac. Perhaps it is, or perhaps women, too, are attracted to the aura of power. Whatever be the reason, many *goonda*s and dacoits I have encountered in my career have been particularly fond of female company. Banda's notorious *goonda* Lalta Singh was no exception. He was the son of a serving police officer, who was at that time posted in Allahabad. Every bus running between Banda and Allahabad would have to keep two front seats vacant just in case he decided to travel that day to meet his parents. The cinema halls of the city used to oblige him and his friends to see any movie in any show free of cost. Every month, he would extort money from every shopkeeper in the city in return for ensuring their businesses ran 'smoothly'. His father was very influential because he was reputed to be close to a powerful cabinet minister. But Lalta Singh also had a roving eye, and this eventually proved to be his downfall.

One day, a senior counsel came to my office. He told me that Lalta Singh had tried to molest his wife. Unfortunately, he didn't want to file a complaint since it would bring disrepute to his family. I wanted to do something, but my hands were tied as the man refused to register a case.

But god has his own way of dishing out justice.

In the evenings, I would sometimes go to the club to play

badminton. Often, after our matches, we would sit down for a cup of tea and have a chat. One of the youngsters I played with was Bhuvan. He would listen intently when I would tell them they were all policemen without uniform, and all policemen were citizens in uniform. I told them that they had a right to defend themselves and their property if a criminal attacked them or any other person in sight. Members of the public had a right to arrest a proclaimed offender or an absconder. All this was especially important here, as the law and order situation had been so bad.

Bhuvan's family was highly educated and cultured. They also happened to be Lalta Singh's next-door neighbours. Lalta Singh's roving eye chanced upon Bhuvan's elder brother's wife. He would follow her around and was waiting for an opportunity to have his way with her. The opportunity arose when one day the other family members were away from the house. Lalta Singh climbed down the tiled roof of the neighbour's house and jumped into the front lawn. Then he pounced on the poor woman. Fortunately for her, Bhuvan came and saw what was happening. What happened next created a sensation.

My doorbell rang at around midnight. The sentry said that a frightened young man with a gun wanted to speak to me. I told him to seat the young man in my office and take the gun from him. It turned out to be Bhuvan.

'Bhuvan, what happened? What brings you here at this odd hour?' I enquired.

He was shivering and had turned pale.

'Bhuvan, are you all right?' I was tense now.

'Sir, Lalta Singh attacked my *bhabhi* (sister-in-law),' he said. I was disgusted at the man's behaviour.

'Sir, Lalta Singh attacked my *bhabhi*...and...,' he started crying.

'Bhuvan, look at me... Tell me what happened,' I tried to bring him back to his senses.

'Sir, I have killed Lalta Singh,' Bhuvan blurted out. The boy was shivering. He had just killed the most notorious *goonda* of Banda.

I must confess that I wasn't exactly heartbroken. It was a relief to hear that someone who had been a pain in the neck of the Banda Police was dead. But Bhuvan now needed all my protection. I called Inspector Kotwali and ordered him to lodge a complaint, as per the facts narrated by Bhuvan. He had made a complete confession of his crime as it had occurred. It was very evident from his testimony that he had shot dead Lalta Singh to defend the honour of his *bhabhi*. But the law had to take its own course. He was arrested and produced in court. The case generated a lot of sympathy for Bhuvan, and to be honest, the police were also sympathetic towards him. The court first released him on bail and ultimately acquitted him on the grounds of self-defence, with the motive of preventing the heinous rape of his *bhabhi*.

Only one man was unhappy with the court's verdict and that was Lalta Singh's father. He believed that Banda Police had manipulated the murder of his son and that the accused, Bhuvan, had our blessings. He kept on trying to get the case investigated by the state CID. But he could not make any headway in this and ultimately truth prevailed.

CASTE POLITICS AND BANDA'S YELLOW PRESS

In Banda, as indeed in most of UP, caste was, and sadly continues to be, the fulcrum on which the wheels of society turned. Since I was a Brahmin and had been brought in by Radha Krishan Goswamy, also a Brahmin and a Congressman, I faced great opposition initially from Banda's socialists and the communists. To make matters more difficult for me, Banda's press was also in the hands of the socialists and communists. They wanted to show Radha Krishan Goswamy in a bad light, since he happened to be the home minister, so they ganged up against him, and tried to portray every crime in the district as a caste issue. This tactic, in fact, went against me and created a lot of problems for me. While crimes were sometimes committed because of caste fissures, this wasn't always the case. Banda was a very backward district, riddled with *goonda*s and criminals; some crimes they committed had other motives as well.

I would like to quote a typical example. A dhobi belonging to a Scheduled Caste, lived in a small hut in the interior of a forest. He sold the only land he owned for thirty thousand rupees to pay for his daughter's wedding expenses. A gang of four or five criminals came to his house in the night and demanded he hand over the amount to them. He naturally refused to comply with their orders. They began torturing him. They burnt his fingers one by one. The man, in spite of great pain, didn't comply. Eventually, he was burnt to death. I rushed to the scene of the crime and ordered a massive manhunt for the criminals.

To preempt the press, I invited them to my residence for a conference and gave them the facts of the case. I emphasized to them the fact that the unfortunate man had been looted and murdered not because of his caste, but because the perpetrators had got wind of the fact that he had a sizeable sum of money in his house.

The next morning when the UP assembly was in session, a national newspaper screamed, 'A Harijan Burnt to Death'. The UP assembly was shaken and poor Radha Krishan Goswamy had to face the music. Banda being very badly connected by rail as well as by road, newspapers like those published in Lucknow could not reach us before 11 a.m., and by the time they were distributed across town, it was almost noon. Consequently, I hadn't even read the paper when I received an irate call from the Inspector General of Police (IGP). A Dalit had been burnt alive in Banda, and I had chosen to remain silent! I explained the situation to him, calmed him down and promised to have a report sent to him by the next morning.

In spite of my remonstrating with the press fraternity of Banda, they continued to sensationalize every crime that occurred in this fashion. The biggest culprit was the newspaper, which had a very highly reputed correspondent stationed in Banda—Jamuna Prasad Bose. A true socialist, he was honest and simple. In fact, many referred to him as the Gandhi of Banda. The only chink in his armour was that he was easily misled by others and his writings were always coloured by his perceptions of the social injustice perpetrated by the Indian caste system. Mischievous informers would feed him incomplete stories, which he would sometimes report without verifying.

One fine morning, a sensational news appeared on the front page of the newspaper. It was reported that a young Scheduled Caste girl had been raped and the police had not taken any substantive action. The name of the village and the police station had been mentioned. Again, this led to a furore in Lucknow before we, in Banda, had even read the papers that day.

I asked the circle officer of the area to visit the village, speak to the victim and other villagers and submit a report immediately to me. The report, which had reached my desk within a day, shocked me at first. It said that the incident had indeed occurred, the police had caught the accused— but he was out on bail. Why did the incident not come to my notice? Then the circle officer directed my attention to the date of the incident. It turned out that the newspaper had reported an incident that had taken place over two years ago and carried it without finding out exactly when it had taken place!

I immediately made out a report containing the above facts and sent it to the IGP. The report made sensational reading. The IGP was shocked out of his wits. He telephoned me and advised me to meet the editor of the national daily and apprise him of the case. So that's what I exactly did.

The editor of the newspaper was obviously not happy

when I told him that the news on Banda district appearing in his newspaper was often biased and prejudiced. I stressed that this was happening despite the fact that I had started giving the salient facts about each crime to all the local correspondents. He didn't take me seriously. Did I expect that his correspondent should report everything exactly the way I, a government functionary, wanted it published, he asked. I simply handed over the articles about the girl's rape and the dhobi's murder that had appeared in the newspaper. 'Please investigate both these crimes independently and arrive at your own conclusions,' I said before taking his leave.

Things returned to normal. A couple of months later, Jamuna Prasad Bose came to meet me in my office. He told me that he had lost his job because of me. Apparently, the editor's independent enquiry had revealed that the articles published in the paper had indeed misrepresented the facts. Yet, Bose stressed he bore me no rancour, for I had simply done my job.

Years after I left Banda, he was elected to the UP Assembly and was appointed as a minister in the cabinet of the Janta Party government. In those days, I was posted as the SSP of Allahabad district. I was sitting in my office when a constable announced that a minister had come and wanted to meet me. I asked the constable to usher him in. As the minister walked in, I was taken aback to see that it was none other than Bose! He said that he was en route Banda and simply wanted to stop by to say hello. Not only did he not hold any grudges against me, he said that he admired me for being a good officer and a good human being. I was very touched by his gesture.

BUILDING POLICE MORALE

People like Bose who genuinely praised our work were hard to come by. The rest of the time, policing was, and remains, a largely thankless job. Police personnel often have to spend their waking hours enforcing the rule of law and return to empty barracks with nothing by way of entertainment. Constant criticism from the press and public further erodes their morale, especially in a difficult district like Banda. Consequently, I spent much of my time in the police lines, working to ensure the welfare of the policemen.

Often in the evenings, I would play hockey and football with the men in the police lines. Being proficient in both the sports, I started training young constables. I organized tournaments and soon the Banda police teams in both the sports started doing rather well. This helped in developing the esprit de corps, which had been lacking until then. Regular inspections also ensured that the police lines, hospital and the mess were well-run. In the process, I developed personal rapport with many constables and head constables. This was to become a big asset for me in the months ahead.

In 1973, the UP PAC rose in revolt. The revolt was for the demand of better service conditions. The UP police sympathized with their cause. The army had to be called out to suppress it. There were serious clashes in some places, as a result some persons were killed on both sides and a lot of PAC men and policemen were arrested and dismissed from service. The IGP ordered the SPs of all districts to visit their police lines and enquire about the welfare of their men. But the discipline of UP Police had reached rock bottom. In most police lines, the officers were heckled, sometimes not even allowed to speak.

I also had to address the Banda constabulary. It was very sad that such rancour had been allowed to creep into the police force in the state. I told the policemen of Banda Police that indiscipline in a uniformed force was unacceptable and non-negotiable. It saddened me deeply that the army was being brought to Banda, even though I had reiterated to the government that there was no need for it. There was a compelling reason for this: The first ever police revolt had taken place in the early Fifties in Banda, when the inspector in charge of the police lines ordered his men to surround the residence of the SP and take him hostage. I, however, had full confidence in my men. If anyone had a grievance, I said, I hoped he would be man enough to stand up and explain it to me.

The men unanimously agreed that they had no grievances. Whatever was happening in the rest of UP, the Banda Police was satisfied with their jobs and their quality of life. Most of them had been my partners in the sports field as well as in the operations being conducted every now and then. They saw me as one of their own. Nothing could be more gratifying for me. And to think this had been partly accomplished because the sportsman in me was always looking for opportunities to play! The experience showed me that by simply participating in their lives, an SP could establish lifelong relationships of trust and respect with his men.

I stayed in Banda for a year and a half. Life had only just begun to settle into a rhythm, when out of the blue, I received my transfer orders. I was to proceed to a district I knew little about—Farrukhabad. My DIG was not happy with my transfer. He said that Farrukhabad was a really tricky district and prophesied that the government was sending me from the frying pan into the fire. Thus, began the next phase of my career.

6

CRIME CAPITAL, FARRUKHABAD

Founded by one Nawab Muhammad Khan Bangash after the reigning emperor Farrukhsiyar, Farrukhabad is located north-west of Lucknow and famous for its zardozi work and bridal lehengas. There is an old saying, 'Khara Khel Farrukhabadi', which extolls the purity of Farrukhabadi coins and the integrity of its denizens. But alas, the city was, when I was posted there, anything but *khara* (pure)—it was then a hotbed of criminals, gangsters and dacoits. In fact, people said that if you randomly caught hold of any five people in Farrukhabad, at least one of them would turn out to be in possession of a knife or a country-made pistol! Not for nothing was it labelled the 'crime capital of Uttar Pradesh'.

Farrukhabad district fell in the jurisdiction of the DIG of Kanpur Range. A thorough gentleman and seasoned officer, he was the senior-most DIG in the state and was sweating it out for his promotion. However, he felt that I lacked the requisite seniority and experience needed to manage a difficult and tricky place like Farrukhabad. Officers with greater experience had already failed in the task.

On a cold December evening, my family and I drove into Fatehgarh, the district headquarters and the cantonment area of Farrukhabad. At that time, the Fatehgarh cantonment was being used to house a large number of prisoners of war (POWs) captured during the 1971 Indo-Pak War. We were welcomed at the police guesthouse with the news that a very serious crime had taken place that very day.

A businessman from Kanpur had come to Farrukhabad to collect his dues worth about thirty thousand rupees from various shopkeepers of the city. He was looted and stabbed to death before he could return. The crime was serious, but what bothered me more was the way in which it was narrated to me. It seemed as if the police force themselves believed that with such heinous crimes occurring every day, the crime situation in the district was a tough nut to crack...

A STUNNING WELCOME BY THE CRIMINALS TO THE NEW SP

The day I had gone to take charge as the SP of Farrukhabad was a very cold, chilly and foggy one. Very early in the morning, I was informed about a serious case of dacoity, with a double murder, in a village under Kampil police station jurisdiction by the notorious gang of Sheodan operating in the area. I had asked the police control room to direct all the station officers of the neighbouring police stations to meet me at the scene of crime and left for Kampil immediately.

I reached Kampil and went to the scene of crime. I spoke to the villagers and the local police to ascertain the details of the crime and find out which way the gang had escaped. I ordered the local police to raid all the places that were known for giving shelter to this gang in the past and keep me informed of the progress of the investigation. My DIG wanted to speak to me to know the details of this case. He also spoke to the police chiefs of the neighbouring districts and sought their cooperation against this, and other gangs operational in the area.

Thus ended my first day as the SP of Farrukhabad.

The next morning dawned with the news of another grave crime. Apparently, a big shop of guns, rifles and pistols in the small town of Tirwa on the road going to Kanpur had been burgled. A gang of professional thieves had cut open the shutters of the shop and stolen nineteen weapons and a huge amount of ammunition—enough weaponry to arm three to four gangs! This was very serious. The last thing we wanted was for the lawless gangs of Farrukhabad to be better armed than before. Also, it was worrying that so many crimes were taking place one after the other. Did the criminals here not fear the law at all?

My DIG asked me to meet him in Tirwa. The scene of crime was bang on a busy highway. Even at night, we were told that it was frequented by a lot of vehicles. We spoke to the distraught shop owner. Just then, a couple of local residents came to the DIG. Crime was fast rising in the area, they said. They were feeling insecure and wanted the police to take strong action against the criminals. After the DIG ascertained all the facts, he said that this case must be handled not by us but by the state CID. Even though the case was off my hands, I still had a very big professional interest in it. I was very interested that this case must be detected as it was a special crime committed by professional criminals who commit only similar crimes. I wanted to know who these criminals were, who indulged in such crimes.

The following morning was even more sensational. I was woken up at 5 a.m. with a crash wireless message about a shocking instance of gang violence in Guleria village. The Nathua gang had shot dead eight villagers, kidnapped two Muslim girls and escaped after setting fire to the entire village. The villagers were so terrified that they had started migrating from the village. There could not have been a bigger slap than this on the face of the police administration. To think that this was only my third day in the district!

With great trepidation, I called my DIG to give him this news. He, too, was stunned.

'What are you saying? Are you serious? It cannot be! Eight killed; this is too big a figure. Please check again and let me know,' he said.

I wished the figure was wrong! But it wasn't.

'I am aware that you have been in Farrukhabad for only three days and also that you have had no time to activate the district police. But the rate at which extremely serious cases of crime are taking place is not acceptable at all. The public will raise a hue and cry and will resort to agitations against the inefficiency of the police, which will threaten the law and order situation of the district. You will, therefore, have to produce results very fast,' he told me.

I assured him that I would do my best. Thereafter, I left for Guleria. Before leaving, I instructed the police control room to inform all the station officers of the district to reach Kamalganj police station without losing any time. As I entered the village, people came running to my vehicle. As I got down from my jeep, they started wailing and crying. It was difficult to decipher and understand what they were trying to tell me. I told them to gather at one place in the village so that I could listen to everybody and speak to them collectively.

Several villagers were leaving the village with all their belongings. They didn't want to live in fear any more. I sent some policemen to dissuade them from leaving the village and to request those who had left to come back. Some did start returning but many others insisted on leaving.

The scene of the crime was pitiable. The victims still lay on the ground. Relatives wailed over their bullet-ridden bodies. There was a lingering smell of smoke. Some houses were still smouldering. It was a hellish scene. The families of the two innocent girls who had been abducted by the Nathua gang came to me weeping and begged me to help them get their girls back. Meanwhile, the DIG arrived.

Just as my visibly shaken boss was doing a round of the village, two people came forward. They stated that

Nathua had committed those murders in revenge. The DIG advised that a strong police picket should be stationed in the village for at least a month. He further said that it was very necessary that we achieved some positive result very soon. After he left, I met all the station officers gathered at the police station. The press was there as well.

They bombarded me aggressively with questions, almost as if I were responsible for all these crimes myself. No other SP before me had been given such a chilling welcome by the criminals, one commented. Another said that ever since I'd arrived in the district, it seemed that all the criminals had been given the freedom to operate freely. Was there any police administration left in the district? What was my game plan for dealing with the crime currently rampant in the district? I tried to answer their questions, saying a proper plan would soon be put in place to put an end to the gangs and neutralize all the active criminals. I will make them pay for their crimes with interest.

THE BEGINNING OF THE END

After the DIG left and I got a respite from the press personnel, I lost no time in calling for a meeting of all the station officers already present in Kamalganj. This is something I'd been itching to do but the events of the last few days had not permitted it. At the meeting, we decided that in the absence of any definite information, we simply had to get ears on the ground and try to track down the gangs in the adjacent forests of Shinghirampur. Just then,

I was informed that somebody was waiting outside with some urgent and important information.

It turned out to be a retired head constable who had known me since the time I was posted as ASP of Agra. After retirement, he had moved to his native village in Farrukhabad district, near the forest area of Shinghirampur.

'Today when I was going to my fields early in the morning, I heard the groans of a girl. I found her lying in a pit and crying and writhing in pain. She had a gunshot wound on one of her shoulders...' he said. It could be one of the two girls abducted from Guleria village by the Nathua gang! The retired head constable speculated that the gang, after committing the mass murders, had escaped into the forest of Shinghirampur, and on the way, shot the girl and left her to die. He offered to lead us to the pit where the wounded girl had been lying.

I immediately went back to the meeting and told the officers that this could be a god-sent opportunity. I asked them where the gang would be likely to head for cover if we were to comb the Shinghirampur area. 'There are some Thakurs living there who are known for harbouring criminals.'

I immediately divided the officers and the force available into four parties. Each of these parties consisted of one platoon (about thirty personnel) of the PAC and about twenty police personnel from the district police and was commanded by a deputy superintendent of police (DSP). Three parties would comb the forest area from the left, right and centre. The fourth party was to lie in ambush along

Biting the Bullet

the exit route from the forest heading towards Akhmelpur village. This party was led by Inspector Bhagwati Singh and consisted of just ten PAC personnel, with a LMG group, and five men of the district police chosen by himself.

The plan was simple. We would all first go to the pit to rescue the wounded girl and then comb the forest area towards Akhmelpur. Each party was briefed and provided with a wireless set for swift communication. I was to be in the party combing the centre of the forest.

It was a cold December day. We found the wounded girl in a pitiable condition, crying and writhing in pain. Nearby, there were bags of leftover food, leaf plates and empty bottles, indicating that the gang had probably stopped there for a while. The girl was too weak from the loss of blood to tell us much. But we finally managed to understand that Nathua had wanted to molest her. When she resisted, he shot her and left her in the pit to die. I had her sent to the hospital immediately. Fortunately, she survived.

By then, it was noon. We started the combing operation. My sixth sense told me that the gang was still in the forest. Thus, I kept sending messages to all the parties to tread carefully and be alert, as a chance encounter could take place at any time. We kept advancing towards Akhmelpur.

As the sun was setting and the shadows lengthening, I began to feel restive. It was already 4 p.m., and we simply had to reach Akhmelpur before the onset of darkness. On unfamiliar terrain, we would be at a great disadvantage in the darkness. I began to worry that Nathua and his gang were also aware of this. As it became darker, I also began to worry that my men could be sitting ducks for the gang, who might be hiding in the forest. However, when I voiced these concerns to my men, to my joy they all wanted to continue. I felt very proud of their commitment.

Just then, there were gunshots in the distance, followed by the unmistakable firing of a light machine gun. I was overjoyed because I knew that contact had been established with the gang. The encounter had begun. We hastened towards Akhmelpur and the gunshots became louder. I spoke to all the team leaders and cautioned them to remain very alert. It was possible that some members of the gang, in order to escape the volley of bullets being fired by the ambush party, might try to escape and try to take cover in the forest.

Bhagwati Singh's excitement was palpable even through the crackle of the wireless. He was elated that his plan had worked. As anticipated, the gang had run into their ambush and there had been a brisk exchange of fire from both the sides. After the firing stopped, he had sent out a reconnaissance party to ascertain the outcome. The party reported that two dacoits had been killed, the kidnapped girl had been recovered and some weapons and ammunition had been found.

One of the two killed was the notorious Chunua, reported to be the right-hand man of Nathua. He was also carrying a reward on his head. This was the best start I could have got in my new assignment. I felt very proud of my men, especially of Bhagwati Singh and his men in the ambush party. I promised that they would be rewarded appropriately and started the arduous job of rebuilding the villagers' confidence. The fact that many had fled their homes in fear of Nathua and because they had lost faith in the police, really rankled. This had to change.

We displayed the corpses of the two killed dacoits along with their firearms outside the police station to the public. Once the villagers of Guleria saw these dead bodies personally, perhaps some of their confidence in the police machinery would be restored. Besides the villagers, many passersby also stopped to see them.

My DIG was extremely pleased with the news. Nathua had been effectively restrained and this was something no other SP had managed to accomplish till now. For me, the icing on the cake was that he acknowledged that I had proven myself to be the right choice as the SP for the dicey Farrukhabad district. I felt as if a burden was off my shoulders. The next day, the DGP of UP congratulated me as well. Praise from the chief of the force sent my morale skyrocketing!

NATHUA'S END

Nathua had been stunned by the encounter and the loss he had suffered. For the first time, his supremacy had been challenged. He decided to stay away from Farrukhabad and take shelter in its adjoining districts. His reign of terror had ended, and I entrusted the responsibility of dealing with him and his remaining gang members to the circle officer (DSP) of Kannauj. One day, when Nathua, after quite some time, decided to visit a village in the Gursahaiganj police station area, he was gunned down in an encounter with the circle officer of Kannauj and his team.

As for me, I had to deal with two more strong gangs, who were a thorn in the flesh of the district police. While dreaded dacoits Jarman Singh and Sheodan Kachhi and their gangs were still active, I could not afford to rest on my laurels.

7
THE RISE AND FALL OF JARMAN SINGH

Hardly forty-eight hours had passed after our successful encounter with the Nathua gang. I was back in office, working on strategies to bring career criminals Jarman Singh and Sheodan Kachhi to justice. They were wreaking havoc in the district every day, and while they were active, the region was a tinderbox that could ignite anytime. While I was brainstorming with my men, the telephone rang. To my surprise, the person on the other end was the CM of UP!

Hemwati Nandan Bahuguna was one of the most powerful leaders Uttar Pradesh had seen. He was then a confidante of Indira Gandhi, who had him appointed as the CM of UP at a time when the state and its machinery were passing through a very difficult phase. The UP Police had risen in revolt in 1973. The treasury of the state was almost empty. Bahuguna was a good choice for the post. Known for his clear thinking and sound governance, he was an able administrator who had perfected the art of extracting work from others. This is exactly what he was doing today.

'We have heard a lot of good things about you from the DGP. I've personally called you today to ask you to end the menace of the dreaded gangster Jarman Singh. He has been operating since the last few years and his terror has gripped the whole area,' he said.

He revealed that the assembly elections were round the corner and the Congress Party wanted to field some able candidates from Farrukhabad and its environs.

'But Jarman Singh has announced that if the ticket is given to any non-Yadav, he or she will be shot dead. Consequently, even candidates who have a good chance of being elected, but do not belong to Jarman's community of Yadavs, are refusing to file their nominations!' he told me.

This was a challenge to the democratic process of the country, he said. Bahuguna's government had decided to put an end to Jarman Singh's reign of terror. Since the elections were less than six months away, he gave me a window of barely three months to achieve this task. Although he offered me every possible aid from the state, the task seemed Herculean.

When I hung up the phone, I wished there was someone I could speak to. To say that I was taken aback would be an understatement. It was not usual for the CM to forego protocol and directly talk to an officer as junior as me.

He had simply ordered me to neutralize a formidable and powerful gang like that of Jarman Singh in less than three months because it was a political requirement. But how would I do it?

THE STORY OF JARMAN SINGH

Jarman Singh, as mentioned earlier, was from the Yadav community. Traditionally, they have been mainly a non-elite, pastoral caste mainly engaged in raising cattle. Members of this community claim descent from the mythological king Yadu (also said to be the forefather of Lord Krishna). In those days, and even today in UP, this community is highly unified and integrated. This posed a big problem for me as this was a predominantly Yadav belt and nobody was willing to rat Jarman Singh out. Instead of being perceived as a criminal and a fugitive from justice, he was seen as a demigod and enjoyed the protection of his entire community.

Jarman Singh belonged to village Balampur in district Mainpuri, which borders the district of Farrukhabad. Apparently, he would move about freely without the fear of the police in a number of villages in this area. He knew that if anyone betrayed him, they would be seen as having betrayed their entire community.

There was only one thing I could do to start. I held a meeting.

All the officers of the district were unanimous in their view that getting reliable information on Jarman Singh in Farrukhabad was next to impossible. So I took a team to

Mainpuri, his birthplace, to see if we could get any leads there. The town of Mainpuri was very backward and underdeveloped. The SP of Mainpuri was helpful but also believed that nobody in his district would have the guts to inform on Jarman Singh as most of them were from his community and under his protection.

Even after six weeks in Farrukhabad, I had not found a single lead to Jarman Singh's whereabouts! It was evident that I needed to think out of the box...

LAYING THE TRAP

On my return, I directed all the station officers and circle officers to map out all the villages where Jarman Singh had been seen in the past or where he was known to have taken shelter. Then I asked all the officers to mark out the shortest routes from their police stations to these villages and study possible escape routes that Jarman Singh could use. These were possible sites where our teams could lie in ambush. Further, I instructed each concerned station officer to nominate a very able and reliable police constable who was well versed with local routes to guide the police team tracking the gang. Discretion, I emphasized, was critical. Jarman Singh, with his wide range of informants and sympathizers, should not get wind of the fact that we were planning anything special for him.

Next, I met the DM who had been posted there for enough time for him to develop solid insights into the area's politics. He was a capable and mature administrator, whose advice about difficult issues was usually sound. Our discussion revealed that a politician from the city constituency could be a useful source of information. Unlike many other *neta*s in the area, he was well-educated and was reputed to always have the welfare of the district in mind. I realized that I would benefit by exchanging views with him, so I invited him to tea.

Niceties exchanged, I quickly brought the conversation to the subject of the gangs of Farrukhabad. We discussed the gang of Sheodan Kachhi first. A rumour was going around the city that he had been visiting the city with a view to kidnap a rich businessman. This had caused a lot of fear, especially amongst the richer residents of the city. Then we finally came to the subject of Jarman Singh, and the problems he was posing for the Congress Party in the upcoming elections. I told him I'd hit a roadblock in getting any information about him. Did he have any suggestions about how I could move forward in my mission to nab the dacoit and his gang?

Politicians will always be politicians. He smiled and said nothing. I, again, goaded him and requested him to think. Perhaps he'd like to take some time to rack his brains, I suggested. Eventually, he said that he would tell me something on the condition of absolute secrecy. I gave him my word.

'How much do you know about Brijender (name changed)?' he asked.

Ajai Raj Sharma

OUR FIRST LEAD

Brijender was from the Mohammadabad area and had been in politics for a long time. From humble origins (his father owned a few *bigha*s of land, a couple of bullocks to plough his fields and a couple of milch cattle), he had risen to a position of high power and wealth.

'Brijender now possesses hundreds of *bigha*s of agricultural land, a transport company, a cold storage and a degree college. He is now a rich man by all standards. Yet, as far as I know, he doesn't even pay income tax!' he said. 'Most interestingly, I'm told that Jarman Singh respects him highly. In fact, whenever they meet, Jarman Singh touches his feet...' Brijender's son lived in a separate house in the area. It was said that whenever Jarman Singh was in the vicinity, he would have a meal with him.

This was the first good lead I'd had and I was elated. The politician cautioned me that Brijender was a nasty politician with tremendous nuisance value. I had a difficult task ahead, he said, and must tread carefully.

After he left, I made inquiries into Brijender's reputation and the picture that emerged wasn't pretty. From all accounts, he was a bully, blackmailer and would probably not respond well to an aggressive approach from a police officer. Perhaps I needed to try something different. I telephoned him one day and enquired about his general welfare. He seemed flattered and pleased to hear from me. In order to establish a personal equation with him, I praised him fulsomely for his role in the development of the district.

Biting the Bullet

After a cordial chat, I hung up, satisfied at having established contact. In the meantime, on my orders, the intelligence unit was gathering information about Brijender—him and his family's finances, assets and list of contacts.

Simultaneously, I was scanning the police personnel in the two concerned police stations for dependability, performance and fitness levels. They would be, in the coming months, my first line of defence. I also requested DIG Kanpur Range to allot three additional companies of the PAC for my district. The firepower of the PAC is much superior to that of the district police. They have superior long-range rifles and semi-automatic weapons as well. The idea was to locate additional force at strategic points near the operational area so that they would be available for action at very short notice.

Once I had enough intelligence on Brijender, I invited him to meet me in my office. Was there any particular problem, he asked cautiously. I replied that the meeting was only to discuss some problems related to the district and his experience in public life could prove helpful. My plan to directly ask him to help the police nab Jarman Singh was audacious—it could provoke Brijender into turning against me. Or, it could push him into a corner and force him to give us information.

He arrived for the meeting on time. I welcomed him with a cup of tea. After some initial chit-chat, I asked him what he knew about the gangs operating in this region. It was, I told him, at the behest of the CM that I had trained my sight on Jarman Singh's gang. Ordinary people had too much to lose by turning into police informers—but perhaps Brijender could help us.

Brijender was squirming in his chair. Clearly, this line of conversation had taken him by surprise. He had no way of helping us catch a criminal as ferocious as Jarman Singh, he said. He went on to add that even his movement in his own constituency would become very difficult if he tried to provide us information against Jarman Singh. It was widely believed, I pointed out, that the gangster respected Brijender as a political leader. Surely, he wouldn't come to any harm, I exclaimed!

The time for beating around the bush was over. Many people in the district, I told him, believed that Jarman Singh was in touch with him and recognized him as the most important political leader in the region. He was taken aback, and he gave me the impression that perhaps I was expecting too much from him. He immediately asked what I expected from him. Could he convince Jarman Singh to lay down his arms and surrender to the police, I asked. Brijender blustered that he could do no such thing. I pulled out a copy of the intelligence report we'd gathered on him. The report mentioned that his son had wined and dined with Jarman Singh. Brijender flew into a fury and threatened to use his contacts to have me transferred in a day's time. I replied that he could do what he wanted, but he should keep in mind two facts. One was that the CM himself was very keen for the liquidation of the Jarman gang. Second, if he didn't cooperate, I would be at liberty to make the facts in the report public. These could cause him serious political damage. He stormed out, leaving me to think that I might have blown my first good lead. But something unexpected happened. I heard the sound of footsteps.

'SP sahib, you have caged me now. Tell me, what is to be done?' he asked.

I smiled and sent for two cups of tea.

PLANTING A MOLE IN JARMAN SINGH'S GANG

As we had not been able to find any locals willing to give information about Jarman Singh, only one option remained. We had to plant a mole within his gang with Brijender's help. My job was to find someone with the presence of mind and bravery needed for such an assignment; Brijender's job was to figure out how to get him in.

Who could I induct into this assignment? He would have to be intelligent enough to quickly enter into his inner circle, make himself indispensable and win the gang's confidence. Using Brijender as the go-between, he would relay information to the police. It was risky. It was unthinkable even. But we were desperate to get our man.

Through a contact who was having an affair with a famous Thakur politician from the Congress Party who was being threatened by Jarman Singh, I finally found a candidate. He introduced me to an enterprising twenty-four-year-old Lakhi, whose family he knew well. Lakhi had, of late, fallen into bad company, was wanted in a case of attempt to murder and was now absconding. If Lakhi helped the police by becoming the mole they so desperately needed, would the police in turn help him? Further questioning revealed that Lakhi had been charged with a crime that he had not committed. Since the police wanted to arrest him, he had thought it was better to abscond. Since he was in hiding from the police, I met him in secret and assured him that if he carried out the task at hand, I would ensure that the charge of attempt to murder levelled against him would be dropped. Thereafter, he would be a free man to live with his family. Besides, he would also get a handsome monetary reward. Within two days, he was ready to accept my offer.

'Are you absolutely sure?' I asked Lakhi. The mission would be a dangerous one. To my joy, Lakhi's decision was in the affirmative. We decided to get Lakhi into Jarman Singh's gang as a member as well as his personal servant. Lakhi would have to cook his food, massage his body and take care of his personal comforts—that too well enough to endear himself to his boss in the shortest possible time. In fact, he would have to try to make Jarman Singh totally dependent on him. While executing his duties, Lakhi had to observe the habits of not only his boss, but of each member of the gang. It was indeed a difficult and dangerous task; it was imperative that he stayed alert all the time. I assured him that the case against him would be dropped. God forbid, if anything happened to him, his family would be looked after by us and would be provided with sufficient money so that they could take care of themselves. Only one thing remained before we asked Brijender to introduce Lakhi into Jarman Singh's gang. We needed to give him a decent weapon not just to defend himself, but also because that would ease his entry into the gang. He told me that he already possessed an illegal rifle.

Everything now depended on Brijender and Lakhi's performance. All we could do was wait and watch. I handed over two thousand rupees to Lakhi for his expenses and wished him all the best in his mission.

Thereafter, Brijender and Lakhi left.

THE BEGINNING OF THE END

Waiting is perhaps the most difficult part of police work. Faced with the prospect of simply twiddling my thumbs while waiting to hear if our mole had been successfully planted, I decided to visit all the police stations that were likely to be involved in the Jarman Singh operation. The idea was to assess the morale and fitness of the policemen who could be involved in it, if and when it took place. For the same reason, I also visited the PAC detachments strategically located in the operational area. I located myself in a government guest house close to the operational area. The guest house was strategically located and would serve as the control room whenever the action began. All the maps we'd prepared earlier, along with all the communication equipment and some additional PAC force under a competent district police officer, would be in the control room.

Meanwhile, Brijender introduced Lakhi to Jarman Singh and sang his praises. He suggested that Lakhi would not only be a useful addition to the gang, he would also look after him personally. No sooner had Lakhi been introduced to the gang, he, as per the written script, devoted himself to the gang in general, and Jarman Singh in particular. Very soon, he won over the confidence of Jarman Singh and became his Man Friday. Lakhi's rifle proved to be an asset for him. It helped Jarman to easily accept him as a regular member; a member who could cook, wash clothes, massage his body whenever he was physically tired, and when the need arose, use his rifle effectively. Jarman Singh Yadav could not have asked for more.

Once Lakhi had become a part of the gang, I felt as if 80 per cent of the mission had been accomplished. Each passing day was full of expectancy. I knew it was only a matter of time now. But the lull before the storm was particularly hard. I found myself beset with doubts. What if Lakhi failed, or still worse, what if he double-crossed us? I felt restless and uneasy.

But Lakhi proved to be a man of his word. One fine morning, my telephone operator woke me up. He said that Brijender was on the line.

'Your friends are coming for half a day, so you should come to the guest house to meet them soon,' he said cryptically.

Our wait was over! I immediately left for the guest house and issued orders on the wireless to all concerned in the operational area to be alert and ready. I also directed the circle officer of Mohammadabad to come to the guest house. Brijender was waiting when I reached the guest house. He told me that about three hours back, Lakhi had informed him that Jarman Singh, along with a few members of his gang including Lakhi, were planning to visit the village Sambalkha. Jarman Singh had been asked to resolve a serious land dispute between two Yadav families, both close to him. In this part of the country, land disputes were often settled by outlaws. Jarman had agreed to their request and informed them that he would reach their village around 2 p.m. This was excellent actionable intelligence.

I immediately summoned all the three station officers, two circle officers and two PAC officers of the operational area and asked them to prepare to surround Sambalkha. They must cover all the escape routes from the village and have ambush parties well camouflaged on each of them. I also directed them to ensure that the control room was kept informed of their locations all the time.

The plan was for all the teams to act simultaneously. Zero Hour was 1430 hours.

It was finally time for action.

TIME FOR ACTION

All we had to do was wait for Jarman Singh and his men to arrive in Sambalkha and hopefully fall into the trap we'd laid for them. All sorts of worries and misgivings were plaguing me. What if Lakhi double-crossed us? What if Jarman Singh got wind of our plan?

Fortunately, my negative thoughts were proved wrong.

Lakhi did not double-cross us; instead, it was Jarman Singh who fell into the trap. He reached the village and was arbitrating the property dispute. Meanwhile, Zero Hour approached.

One of the parties led by the station officer of Nawabganj police station was spotted by a gangster who was on the roof of a house and keeping a lookout. He immediately sounded an alarm, and, in fact, fired a couple of shots, even though the policemen were out of the range of his fire. From my posting in the Chambal region, I had acquired a first-hand experience of the reaction of gangs when they are being surrounded by the police. Their first reaction is not to allow the police to complete their cordon. In case it has been completed, they then try to break it and escape. Unfortunately for them, in this case, they were almost surrounded. Even the ambush parties were in the process of taking their respective positions. Through wireless communication, I sent a word to all the police parties to hold fire. I directed them not to fire until and unless their target was fully in their firing range and fully visible to them.

This way, the gang would not be able to assess easily where all of us were located. Once the attack party went into action and attacked the exact position where Jarman Singh was located, the gang started escaping by running out of the village. It turned out that only five gang members were with Jarman Singh at that time. He immediately broke up his group into two, and they went off in different directions. The group without Jarman Singh tried to escape to the western side of the village, which had a lot of shrubbery and tree cover. In the other group, Jarman Singh was instantly identifiable. He was much taller than the rest and was dressed in military fatigues. He and his men tried to take shelter in some dilapidated *kachha* huts on the eastern side of the village.

The police team could see the three gangsters running towards these huts and fired at them. Since their target was out of their range, they could cause no harm to the escaping gangsters. As they closed in, these dacoits also fired back. The policemen, being in the open, had to take up crawling positions for their protection. The cross-firing between the two carried on for some time. I realized from the messages I was getting in the control room that the police firing was of no use. Hence, I sent a direction to them to send a group of about five constables under the command of an SI, to flank the gang from the rear.

This group launched an attack even while the attack party had the gang constantly engaged from the front. Meanwhile, I was getting all the information through the wireless in the control room. I sent a message to the circle officer of Mohammadabad to send a party with LMGs from the nearest PAC detachment to strengthen the attack party. The group behind the gangsters had almost reached within firing range and could see the movements of small figures in and out of the huts. Almost at the same time, reinforcements with LMGs arrived in the front. Now Jarman Singh was sandwiched. Both groups started firing together and he began to feel the heat.

The rapid rate of fire from the LMGs unnerved the three gangsters. Unable to handle this new situation, Jarman Singh realized he needed an alternate way to escape. To his south, at a distance of about hundred metres, he saw a vast crop of sugarcane spread over a huge area. All three gangsters spread out and started crawling for the fields of tall sugarcane. This helped them cover some distance without being noticed. On the way, wherever they could, they sprinted behind the cover of shrubs and bushes. For a short while, the police parties were foxed by this move. All they could see were tiny figures appearing, then disappearing in the bushes. But Jarman Singh did not know what lay in store.

A police party was lying in ambush inside the sugarcane fields. As soon as Jarman Singh reached the shelter of the sugarcanes, they opened fire. A volley of bullets hit him and he fell.

'Task achieved. Jarman Singh killed,' crackled the wireless. Sitting in the control room, a huge wave of emotion passed through me when I heard the news. The teams had managed to accomplish what nobody else had been able to do. I asked the control room to send a crash message to the DIG of Kanpur and DGP of UP and hastily left for the scene of the encounter.

A TRAGEDY UNFOLDS...

At the time when I was hurrying towards village Sambalkha, a tragic event was simultaneously taking place. The two gangsters who had separated from Jarman Singh's group had not yet been caught. When they heard the sound of firing, they decided to run away from the village.

Biting the Bullet

The gangsters ran past the house of a Thakur family who had been great enemies of Jarman Singh, because the Thakurs had a great rivalry with the Yadavs of the area. Two of the family members had retired from the army and possessed licensed weapons. When they heard that the police had surrounded Jarman Singh and an encounter was going on, they picked up their weapons and mounted their horses, ready to join the encounter. When they saw the two gangsters trying to escape, they gave chase. One of the fleeing gangsters tripped and fell. The Thakur men immediately pinned him down while the other gangster escaped.

It was Lakhi, the brave mole without whom this mission would never have been possible. He begged the Thakurs to spare his life. When he realized they were in no mood to listen to him, he even told them that he had joined the gang on my behest. He entreated them to verify this fact from me. Bloodlust overtook the two Thakurs, and they shot him dead from point blank range.

Meanwhile, I had reached the sugarcane fields where Jarman Singh lay. He was a handsome man with a chiselled face, impressive moustache and a muscular physique. A small silver idol of goddess Durga was found tied around his waist. In his pocket, there was quite a lot of cash. I was quite overcome as I looked at his now peaceful face. Here lay a man who once threatened the whole political system! A man who had let loose a reign of terror that totally destroyed the peace and calm of the people living in this region...

The news of Jarman Singh's death spread like wildfire. All

the villagers belonging to the nearby areas started arriving to get one last glimpse of their demigod. Amongst them were Brijender and his son as leaders of the Yadav community. Our eyes met secretly. He shed a few crocodile tears for the sake of his constituency and left.

Operation Jarman Singh had been an outstanding success. The only dark cloud on the horizon was the tragic killing of Lakhi. He lay where he had fallen, his eyes wide open. It seemed he was looking into the future he had dreamed of, a new life that we had promised him for playing his part. The two Thakur brothers were bragging over his dead body, telling everyone how they had killed one of the gangsters. I told them that Lakhi was certainly not a dacoit and had been planted into the gang by me. I became emotional when I told them that today's success had been possible only because of the risk he had undertaken. But what had been done could not be undone.

It was already six in the evening, and I had to reach Kanpur. My DIG had been promoted and transferred. The SPs and SSPs of Kanpur Range, including me, were hosting a farewell dinner for him. Upon my arrival, I was greeted with garlands and flowers. My outgoing boss was thrilled at the success his team had achieved and that too on his last day in office. In his farewell speech, he praised me handsomely and wished me well.

I felt a little lost and unable to really enjoy the party. Perhaps it was because in my mind's eye, I could still clearly see the valiant Lakhi smiling at me confidently before he left for the mission that cost him his life...

8

THE DREADED GANGSTER SHEODAN KACHHI

They say that a police officer's job is never quite done. I certainly felt that way in Farrukhabad! For even though we had worked tirelessly to end Nathua and Jarman Singh's reigns of terror, crime in Farrukhabad district just did not let up. The dreaded gangster Sheodan Kachhi continued to commit robberies and murders with impunity across the district. Unlike Nathua and Jarman Singh, this bandit operated in the northern portion of the district, which bordered the districts of Etah, Badaun and Shahjahanpur. It was reported that he also visited the districts of Hardoi and Mainpuri only for the purpose of seeking shelter, but never committed any crime in these districts.

Sheodan belonged to the Kaimganj area of Farrukhabad district and was Kachhi by caste. The Kachhi are, by and large, a poor community often to be found working as farm labourers. Sheodan also grew up in poverty. Although Kaimganj was an agriculturally prosperous area, it was prone to crime, particularly because it bordered Aliganj, a hub for hardened criminals and gangsters. In his younger years, Sheodan was involved in petty crimes. He was attracted to the Robin Hood-like persona of many notorious gangsters of that time. The police warned him several times to desist from indulging in petty crimes and anti-social activities.

It was not long before Sheodan formed his own gang with four members and acquired a few country-made weapons. The gang committed petty robberies and successfully evaded arrest by taking shelter in the neighbouring districts of Etah, Badaun and Shahjahanpur. With the money he got from petty crime, Sheodan purchased sophisticated firearms, including a sten gun for himself, which I learnt belonged to some army unit. He also started carrying a foreign-made double-barrelled 12-bore gun.

Armed with such weapons, his sadistic nature came to the fore.

MURDER, MAYHEM AND SADISM...

It soon became apparent that with every successive crime, Sheodan seemed to derive sadistic pleasure from his victim's pain.

In a bizarre case, his gang surrounded a few houses in a village. One of the gang members climbed on to a rooftop. Panic-stricken villagers recall that he started playing a drum and singing a popular Hindi song, *'Maar diya jaye ya chhor diya jaye'* (Should you be killed or spared?) The gang, meanwhile, went from house to house, looting cash and terrorizing the families. Two young men tried to intervene. The gangsters took them to Sheodan. He flew into a rage and repeatedly hit them with the butt of his gun till they were half dead. Then he ordered his men to finish them off before the eyes of the terror-stricken villagers. Even after they were shot dead, Sheodan wasn't quite done.

He ordered the widows of the two men to be brought out and forced them to dance around their husbands' dead bodies. The poor women were in no condition to comply with these cruel orders. But they had to when Sheodan started whipping them.

When I heard of this incident, I was reminded of a Bollywood blockbuster. But this was no movie—this was what Sheodan had become in real life! The news of this dastardly crime spread like fire in the neighbouring villages and districts, creating more fear in the entire rural belt and neighbouring cities. His gang rose from strength to strength and their infamy reached its zenith when Sheodan started killing even police personnel, that too in full view of the public. The most sensational of these cases was when he killed two policemen who were returning from Fatehgarh in a bus. He stopped the bus, brought the two constables out, tied them to a nearby tree and shot them in public view. Matters came to a head when he threatened to kill the MLA of Aliganj. The MLA belonged to the Congress Party, which was at that time the ruling party. The frightened

MLA entreated the state government to curb this menace. The government declared a huge reward on Sheodan's head.

As SP of Farrukhabad, the task of neutralizing this sadistic dacoit fell on me. By now, I had evolved a loose strategy for tracking dacoit gangs. First, I asked all the station officers and the circle officers of the area to brief me about the activities of Sheodan and his gang. I also asked each of them to draw up a list of all their known contacts. The next step was to pressurize all the contacts identified, in the hope that one of them would break and opt to turn into an informant.

The raids conducted by the police created a lot of flutter in all the villages, which had been frequented in the past by Sheodan and his gang members. When all his known contacts were interrogated for hours, even days at the police station, villagers were even more astonished. Such an exercise had not been undertaken in the past and sent Sheodan the message that the police meant business. Then we learnt that he had started hiding in neighbouring districts to escape the Farrukhabad Police.

THE HUNTER BECOMES THE HUNTED

One day, I received an inland letter written in Hindi. It was poorly written, seemingly by someone not very well educated. It was from Sheodan himself!

In the letter, he wrote that he was aware of my plans to arrest or kill him. Since he had a great deal of respect for me, he wanted to warn me off. If I harmed him or any of his gang members, he would retaliate by kidnapping my two young sons. Sheodan had clearly had my family under surveillance as he went on to say that he knew which school they went to, and that they went every day in a white Fiat car with the registration number USB 555. He ended by saying that by kidnapping my children, he would bring me to my knees. It would be much better, he advised, if I sought a transfer to some other district.

Until I was sure that the letter was authentic, I did not want to upset my wife with it. Fortunately, the DIG of Kanpur Range arrived in Fatehgarh a day later. He was J.N. Chaturvedi, a seasoned, intelligent and capable officer. Years later, he became the first commissioner of police, Delhi, and thereafter, the DGP of Uttar Pradesh. During his stay in Fatehgarh, I informed him about the letter from Sheodan and showed it to him. After reading the letter, he was somewhat sure that the letter had been written by Sheodan himself. We had to take the threat seriously. The DIG spoke to my wife, suggested certain security measures. He also wanted the implementation of stricter security measures when the children were in school.

Ensuring more security for my family, I returned to the task at hand with renewed enthusiasm. We started pursuing a different line of action. Since we had not had much success in finding reliable informants, perhaps we could turn one of Sheodan's gang members, to succeed against him. I asked all the concerned police officers to provide me with detailed information about every member of the gang—family, financial status, educational background, friends and acquaintances and their peculiarities and quirks. Upon examining the information, I surmised that there was only one dacoit we had some chance of breaking.

His name was Babu.

OPERATION BABU

Before becoming a dacoit, Babu had worked as a conductor in a transport company based in Kaimganj. The company belonged to Miyan, a Pathan, whose ancestors had come from Afghanistan years ago and settled in Kaimganj. Miyan earned enough money from his transport business to buy a fair amount of land and earn respect not only in Kaimganj, but also in the neighbouring areas. Perhaps we could induce Miyan to work with the police and convince Babu to become an informer...

But how?

We had to do something to induce Miyan to seek *my* help. We decided to use his twenty-year-old son, Miraj as a pawn. Miraj was Miyan's weakness, and everyone knew that the adoring father would do anything for his son. Miraj had recently acquired a motorcycle and loved racing it. Kaimganj was a mofussil town with narrow roads. Thus, speeding in the lanes of Kaimganj was dangerous, especially for pedestrians. I appointed the dashing Inspector Himmat Singh the head of Kaimganj police station, who always boasted of being a Thakur, who keep their word. He also used to tell me that if ever a need arose he could make any sacrifice for me. His task was that after a couple

Biting the Bullet

of weeks, he should take overtly aggressive action against Miyan's son for rash and negligent driving. It should not be an ordinary challan.

I knew that being a Pathan, Miyan would prize his prestige and dignity above everything else. Sure enough, when Himmat Singh hauled up Miraj in public and took him by the scruff of his neck to the police station, Miyan was infuriated. He immediately went to the police station and threatened the inspector with dire consequences. He publicly announced that he would meet me and request for Himmat Singh's transfer.

The die was cast.

Miyan was brought to my office and had a litany of complaints against Himmat Singh. I was already prepared for his demands and apologized for what had happened. The action taken by the police against Miraj had indeed been harsh, I said soothingly. I said that we would conduct an inquiry, and if his allegations were found to be correct, Himmat Singh would be transferred and would have to undergo departmental action. Miyan was a bit surprised that I agreed to all his demands. He left, feeling rather beholden to me, which is exactly what we had aimed for.

As per our plan, we then conducted an inquiry. With a pang of guilt, I issued the transfer orders of Inspector Himmat Singh. As I had explained to him earlier, this was necessary for the larger plan to succeed. And succeed it did. After a period of time, I reinstated Inspector Himmat Singh as a station officer of another police station.

Miyan was filled with joy when he heard the news. He

came to me to convey his gratitude for what he thought to be the restoration of his lost dignity and respect.

'I don't know how to thank you,' he cried. 'Henceforth, I am your slave. Even if you desire my life, I shall be obliged to give it to you!' Little did he know that he had walked into a trap that I had laid for him...

THE BUILD UP

A few days went by without any unusual incident. Sheodan and his gang appeared to be lying low somewhere in one of the neighbouring districts.

One day, Latoori Singh, an MLA from Aliganj, a subdivision of Etah district, and Sheodan happened to cross each other. Latoori Singh had serious differences with Sheodan, who had on one occasion fired at him. When the dacoit and the MLA came across each other yet again, matters got heated. Sheodan threatened to kill him.

A frightened Latoori Singh complained to the UP governor about the fresh threat from Sheodan. Why had the UP Police failed to apprehend Sheodan, even though he had been spreading terror since the last six or seven years? The governor did what governors do—he summoned the DGP and vented his ire. In turn, the DGP hauled up the police chiefs of all the concerned districts. Each SP was asked about the problems they had in taking strong action against the gang. Other than me, they all replied there was no way of getting information against the gang. They all asked for more PAC personnel. When it was my chance to speak, I surprised everyone by saying I did not require any additional force.

After the meeting, I told my DIG that we had a good chance of winning over an important informer. More PAC personnel could alert Sheodan that something was afoot. He was happy with the plan, but cautioned me that time was running out.

MIYAN PLAYS HIS PART

I summoned Miyan to my office for a confidential meeting. I told him that I wanted to seek a favour, which, by all standards, was a difficult task. He immediately assured me that it would be his privilege to help me.

I came straight to the point and asked if he knew Babu. Miyan became instantly uncomfortable. Was I referring to the Babu who was a member of Sheodan gang, he asked. I replied in the affirmative. He tried to prevaricate but I persisted. Finally, he admitted that Babu used to work for him years ago in his transport company. One fine day, he disappeared without even informing Miyan that he was leaving the job. Miyan now helped his elder brother, who was in jail in Shahjahanpur and is under trial in a murder case, every now and then with money.

I told Miyan that I was not leaving Farrukhabad without destroying Sheodan and his gang. I reminded him that I had helped him restore his respect and dignity and now he could not refuse me. He had to help the police by weaning Babu away from the Sheodan gang and convincing him to become a police informer. Miyan protested, saying that the plan would never work. I convinced him to give it his best shot. With the greatest reluctance, Miyan agreed.

A couple of days later, we got our first break.

MIYAN MEETS BABU

I received an urgent message from Miyan saying that he wanted to meet me soon. He seemed somewhat excited when we met. Apparently, he had managed to establish contact with Babu. When they met, Miyan told Babu that his family had been facing several hardships and there was nobody to look after them. Babu replied that he was very aware of this fact, and because of this reason, he often remained worried. He had been away from his family for five years, he said. Miyan asked him if he had ever thought of returning once again to normal life. He told him that the new SP of Farrukhabad Police might be helpful to Babu, if he were properly approached. Babu was surprised: Why would the SP want to help him, he asked. Miyan replied that this could only be known after they had spoken with him.

Babu reminded Miyan that he was a wanted gangster carrying a reward on his head and was wanted in several cases of murder and dacoity. The moment he took the foolish step of meeting a police officer, he either would be shot dead or arrested and put behind bars and spend the rest of his life in jail. Miyan asked him to think about it with a cool head and open mind. He may not get another chance like this one. Babu promised to give it serious thought, saying that he would do so only because he regarded Miyan as someone who truly had his wellbeing in mind.

Time passed quickly. Our deadline approached. Even though I had become better at the waiting game by now, doubts and worries assailed me. What if Babu decided not to meet me at all? Or even worse, what if he met me and rejected my offer? I was mentally very troubled but could not discuss this issue with any of my fellow officers because of the strict secrecy surrounding the operation.

In the meantime, I had to introduce Miyan to the new head of Kaimganj police station, Inspector Raj Kumar Singh, as he was the most important officer for our mission. He was a well-built and soft-spoken man who came across as being very intelligent. As a student of Agra University, he had been a champion athlete as well. After Himmat Singh's orchestrated departure from Kaimganj, Raj Kumar Singh had done well there. But until now, he had no inkling about the role he was going to play in my plan. Swearing him to secrecy, I disclosed the plan to turn Babu against Sheodan and asked him to find the shortest routes to the six villages Sheodan frequented. I introduced him to Miyan and emphasized to both that nobody, other than the three of us, knew about this plan. Secrecy was of essence for the success of the mission and for ensuring Miyan's safety.

RUNNING OUT OF TIME

Our deadline was fast approaching. First, my DIG came on a routine visit and asked about the progress of the case.

Then the DGP summoned a meeting of all the officers of the state. On reaching Lucknow, he sent word that I should meet him before the meeting. He stressed the urgency of nabbing Sheodan and his gang before they wreaked any further damage. Sheodan had become quite a big embarrassment for the government, and the sooner he was brought to justice, the better. I assured him that I would leave no stone unturned to get Sheodan. My confident words belied the anxiety I felt.

Fortunately, two days after my return from Lucknow, Miyan dropped in unannounced at my residence.

'By the grace of Allah, Babu has agreed to meet you,' he said, elatedly. I was relieved to hear this. However, he went on to add, 'But he has a few conditions.'

The conditions were that Babu would not meet me in Farrukhabad where I was the SP. He suggested the name of a village, which was near the border of Kaimganj, but was in the jurisdiction of Aliganj police station in Etah district. The second condition was that the meeting would be one-to-one, between him and me, with nobody else being present. Neither of us would carry a firearm.

These conditions were dicey and were likely to put me in considerable danger. Miyan himself was not very happy with them. He strongly felt that we must properly assess the pros and cons of these terms before agreeing to them. But I felt there was no option but to agree to them, even though they weighed heavily against me.

I told Miyan to fix up the date, time and place for the meeting.

The game was afoot.

Biting the Bullet

THE LONG-AWAITED MEETING WITH BABU

After going back, Miyan managed to contact Babu after four days. Babu was surprised that I had agreed to all his terms. He told Miyan exactly where he wanted us to meet.

The meeting would take place two days from now, at 2 p.m., Miyan informed me.

Miyan returned to Fatehgarh and told me all about his conversation with Babu. As I was not conversant with the route or the area, I asked him to accompany me to the place of the meeting. I would wear plain clothes and use a non-police car for the purpose.

I had two days to think about what I would say to Babu when I met him. I very well understood that this opportunity would not come again; hence, I had to make the best of it. When I apprised Raj Kumar Singh of the plan, he was aghast. Babu was after all a gangster—what if he played foul with me? He suggested that he went in my place. That wasn't feasible, I told him. Babu was expecting to meet the SP of the district and no other officer in his place would do. This was our only chance and we could not allow this opportunity to go. After all, if Babu didn't work out as an informer, we had no other leads to Sheodan.

I simply had to go.

So I told Raj Kumar Singh to reconnoitre the venue of the meeting a day in advance and figure out some vantage points where he, along with three other men of his choice, would be secretly positioned. They should be close enough to be within firing range but far enough so as to not arouse any suspicion. Also, they must wear civil clothes and be appropriately armed. Raj Kumar Singh returned and told me that the meeting site was about five to six hundred metres from the village. He had found an appropriate place where he and his men could hide when the meeting was going on. He left, wishing me good luck for the next day.

The day of the meeting arrived. I was nervous. My wife tried to calm me down. Soon, around 11 p.m., Miyan arrived in the vehicle he had arranged for our rendezvous. En route, we began discussing the possibility of Babu deceiving us. Miyan said that the chances of such an eventuality were miniscule. Yet, because he could not bring himself to rely on a criminal blindly, he had brought his gun and had already studied the meeting spot and found a place to position himself. Babu and I were to meet under an old banyan tree. The faithful Miyan insisted that he would hide himself amongst its dense foliage.

We reached about half an hour before the scheduled time of the meeting and had a quick look around. The village was about half a kilometre away from the spot where we were. Between us and the village, there were fields of newly planted wheat, sown after the paddy crop had been harvested. As the wheat plants were not too tall, we had good visibility. Miyan quickly took his place on the tree.

I waited.

Half an hour later, just as I was beginning to worry Babu may not show up at all, I spotted an individual walking the *kachha* path through the fields. As he came closer, Miyan whistled to alert me and that this was indeed Babu. I tried to observe the individual closely to ascertain if he was carrying a firearm with him.

Babu was wearing a pair of khaki-coloured pants and a brown shirt. He was of medium height and looked to be quite fit. He was walking quite fast and soon he was face to face with me. Introductions were exchanged. Then he came straight to the point.

'What can I do for you?' he asked me.

'I have something important to discuss with you, which is why I had asked for you,' I said.

I am sure Babu knew exactly what I wanted to talk to him about. But he still asked me to tell him the reason for this meeting.

His family was floundering in his absence, I said. His father was dead, his mother was old, his sister was unmarried and his brother was in jail, undergoing a trial in a murder case. They had to keep taking financial assistance from people like Miyan. What would happen, I asked, if he were killed in an encounter and his brother were convicted in the murder case? That was a very likely scenario, one that could play out in the imminent future. Gangsters, in my experience, never had very long lives. How would his mother and sister fend for themselves?

These were negative and disturbing ideas, and I could see the wheels turning in Babu's head. He became disturbed and uneasy. My emotional blackmail had worked. This is exactly the mental state I wanted him to be in when I placed my proposition before him. Meanwhile, sensing he might be able to clinch the deal, Miyan also came out of hiding from the branches of the tree. Babu was surprised. He said immediately that only two people were supposed to be there. Miyan said that he had always been a well-wisher of Babu and his family, and therefore, his presence was essential in the meeting between him and me.

We cut to the chase.

The Sheodan gang had created enough havoc. The government was serious about putting an end to its reign of terror. Miyan explained to him that the idea was that he should help us to nab Sheodan.

The moment Babu heard Sheodan's name he shouted at Miyan: 'Sheodan is my brother; how can I betray him? Before betraying Sheodan, I will kill myself...'

Miyan calmed him down and told Babu that if he did not help us, somebody else would. I intervened and told Babu that I had been assigned the task of liquidating the Sheodan gang, and I was determined to succeed. I told Babu that if he decided to help us, we would have him surrender, send him to jail and ensure that he will not be harmed in any way. I told him that his cases would be dealt with in court on priority basis. He knew as well as I did that witnesses were scared to depose against gangsters like him. Therefore, all cases against him were likely to end in acquittal. He could then go back to his family and start a new life. I would help him with monetary concerns and other necessities to begin life afresh. I told him that Sheodan would be killed eventually, but if that happened without his help, then he would lose the chance of living a new life. He was hesitant.

Babu fell silent. I asked him to imagine a happier future

in which he would be able to live with his mother again, and would be able to get her treatment done and look after her in her old age. He could get his sister married and she would be happily settled in her new family. Perhaps even he could get married and have a family of his own. Wouldn't it be wonderful if he, along with his wife, children and mother could lead a happy life in his village?

The alternative, I pointed out was grim. If he chose to stay with Sheodan and not accept my offer, he could be killed. His dead body would be sent for a post-mortem and then handed over to his mother for cremation. His mother could die of heartbreak. His sister might have to do the unthinkable to survive.

Miyan then took him aside and spoke to him for about fifteen minutes. I could not hear what they were talking about. They came back to me and told me that Babu had finally accepted the offer; he would stay on in the gang and would work for us.

This was the happiest news that I could have got.

THE FINAL COUNTDOWN

I congratulated Babu on his wise decision but added that we only had this month to catch Sheodan. The police forces of five districts were after Sheodan, but since I had worked so hard on tracking him, I wanted to be the one who finished the job. Babu promised to give us actionable information at least six hours in advance. Miyan would relay information back and forth between us.

During the waiting period, Raj Kumar Singh and I planned for the D-day. We estimated the size and composition of the police party. We anticipated the weapons we would require in the very likely eventuality of a shootout. Since there were at best six members in Sheodan's gang, we estimated that a posse of only eight to ten professionally sound and well-equipped police persons would be enough to deal with them.

It was 24 December. I had gone to Shamshabad, which was hardly twenty kilometres from Kaimganj. The Nawab of Shamshabad had become a friend of mine. He used to maintain good relationships with all the important district officials and was a much-respected person of the area. He had invited me for an early dinner. I informed Raj Kumar where I would be present. Fortune seemed to be smiling on me. As we were finishing dinner, Raj Kumar informed me that I must reach Kaimganj immediately. I thanked the Nawab for his hospitality and rushed off to Kaimganj. Raj Kumar was waiting for me eagerly at the destination.

Babu had come through! He had sent us the information that Sheodan, along with his gang, was to reach a village close to his own village at about 2 a.m. on 25 December. There were two Thakur brothers in this village who were eyewitnesses in a murder case against him. He had warned them not to give evidence but they had paid no heed and had the audacity to depose in court against him. Sheodan was going to do what he did best. He was going to kill them.

Raj Kumar Singh had discreetly reconnoitred the route and declared that it was favourable for laying an ambush. He

Biting the Bullet

had drawn out an admirable ambush plan on paper. There was a small hillock on the route and below was the mud track on which the gang would be walking. On the other side of the track, there was a thick growth of cactus-type plants, which were full of thorns. Nearby, there were thickets of tall grasses. No animal or man could easily pass through this natural hedge. The plan was to lay an ambush around the hillock so that the gang would have to pass directly beneath us. We could take on the gang when it was on the dirt path, sandwiched between the high ground and cactus hedge. The topography was such that the ground would give us good protection from the fire of the gangsters.

Once I understood the plan and approved it, each person in the ambush party was briefed about his role in the operation. The whole team was ready to go. Since the sound of our vehicles would have announced our presence, we decided to go on foot. The ambush spot was about four miles from Kaimganj.

We began our march at 11 p.m. in order to be in our positions by midnight. It was bitterly cold, but we were lucky that it was a moonlit night. Jackals howled. The superstitious among our party immediately commented that this was auspicious for us and inauspicious for the gang. The jackals were prophesying that the gang was going to suffer causalities tonight. I hoped they were right.

At the ambush spot, there was good visibility till about sixty yards all around us. I gave all the members in the party ten minutes to break up and make themselves comfortable. Later, they would not be allowed to get up from the ambush for any reason. Once the team reassembled, we formed the ambush. I was in the centre. Five persons lay to my left and formed the head of the ambush. The first person in this group was Raj Kumar Singh. Another five were to my right. This was the tail of the ambush. On my right, just adjacent to me was SI Kaushik. I told Kaushik that when I touched him, he should fire the Very Light Pistol (VLP), which would light up the area for less than half a minute. The group to my left was told to allow the gang to enter the spot and reach the area opposite me. Nobody was supposed to fire till the VLP was fired. The ambush party was covering an area of about forty to fifty yards. We were in full readiness by 0120 hours. And then, we waited patiently to give a warm welcome to Sheodan and his gang members.

It had been arranged with Babu that when the gang was about sixty to seventy yards away, he would light a cigarette and start smoking. This would alert us to the gang's presence. We had also told Babu that he should then announce that he was hanging back to relieve himself. This way, he would avoid being trapped in the ambush along with the other gang members.

Around 0145 hours, we saw the signal of the cigarette light. Then in the moonlight, a shadowy group of four became visible. We all held our breaths as the group entered the ambush and slowly walked right in front of me. As they came to the centre of the ambush, I gave Kaushik the signal. The flare suddenly lit up the night and the gangsters became clearly visible.

Sheodan immediately realized the direction from which

the shot had been fired. He fired a burst of bullets from his sten gun, which hit several places in front of us.

Unfortunately for him, the bright light created by the VLP had given us the chance to aim and fire a volley of bullets at the figures visible to us. The very first bullets fired by us had hit Sheodan. Even after being hit, he fired another burst, but since he lost his balance after being hit, it was of no consequence. One of the members who was walking some yards behind Sheodan, and had not entered the ambush, turned around and fled.

Sheodan had been killed. Another member of his gang, who had been injured, managed to hide himself and got away because of our carelessness. Babu and one other had stayed behind, and surrendered later on.

We quickly went to examine Sheodan as he lay supine on the ground. He had a tattoo of Goddess Durga on one arm, and on the other, a tattoo of his name. On him was his trusty sten gun, one double-barrelled 12-bore gun, several bullets and cartridges and a bag.

We had done it. We had managed to get the gangster who had created a reign of terror in five districts and had been wanted since the last several years. We sent a message for our vehicles, which arrived soon. I asked Raj Kumar Singh to get more SIs from the police station so that all legal formalities before shifting the dead body of Sheodan could be completed as soon as possible. I also asked him to get a photographer from Kaimganj and get photographs taken of the scene of encounter as well as of the dead body of Sheodan.

THE AFTERMATH

Dawn was breaking by the time we returned to the police station. All of us were cold and exhausted. I was dying to break this to my DIG and the DGP but it was too early in the morning to do so. However, the news that Sheodan had been killed spread like wildfire. Even Latoori Singh got the news in his village. He landed up at the Kaimganj police station. He brought baskets full of sweets and distributed them to all the policemen present.

As soon as it was 6 a.m., I could not resist telephoning my DIG at Kanpur. The DIG was thrilled and amazed at our feat. After saying many kind words about me, he said that all the members of our team should be rewarded handsomely. It was still too early for me to call the DGP. To my surprise, he called me in great excitement. When I narrated the entire story to him, he was beside himself. He hung up saying that he had to deliver this good news personally to the governor.

A huge crowd had collected to have a last glimpse of the dreaded Sheodan, who had terrorized them for so many years. Among them was Miyan, who had played such a key role but had cleverly chosen to keep a low profile now that it was all over. I took him aside, expressed my extreme gratitude and told him that all this would not have been possible without him. He was the real hero.

There were many loose ends to be tied up so I left for Fatehgarh. The news about the killing of Sheodan had spread like wildfire throughout the district by then. People kept

Biting the Bullet

flagging me down on the road to greet and congratulate me. In Fatehgarh, I saw to my great surprise that all the MLAs of the district were there to receive me with flowers and garlands. People were standing on either side of the road and were showering petals on us. My wife was visiting her parents in Agra at the time. She, too, was very happy to hear the news. I decided that I, too, would join her in Agra the next morning for a well-deserved break.

Even today, after so many years of retirement, I vividly recall the hero's reception I received that day. I am fortunate to have achieved many more milestones in my career, but the success against the Sheodan gang will always have a very special place in my memory. Ultimately, I was awarded the President's Police Medal for Gallantry (the highest police award), for this effort.

I would like to end the Sheodan episode on a lighter note. Some months later, I was travelling from my hometown Mirzapur to Allahabad in the Howrah-Delhi Express, which is about one and a half hour's journey. Next to me, a co-passenger was reading an article in a popular Hindi magazine *Manohar Kahaniya* with an unusual and catchy headline: '*Kali Nadi Ka Kala Ajgar*' (the Black Python of the Black River). To my surprise, my photograph was next to the headline. I remembered that immediately after the Sheodan encounter, one of the reporters of this magazine had interviewed me in detail. A mischievous thought came to my mind. I asked my co-passenger, 'Whose photograph is this?'

He replied, 'It is of the Superintendent of Police of

Farrukhabad. He has killed the dreaded dacoit Sheodan Kachhi.'

I asked him, 'Doesn't his photograph resemble me? This is the first time I am seeing a photograph of a person who looks a lot like me. Both seem identical.'

He looked at the photograph and then looked at me, and looked at the photograph once again.

'It's true... The photograph really does look like you!'

After this, I kept quiet. The gentleman kept looking at the photograph and comparing it with me. Soon, the train reached Allahabad railway station. A police officer in uniform had come to receive me. He entered the compartment and saluted me.

I said in parting, 'I think he is also confused and thinks me to be the officer in the photograph.'

My co-traveller was standing at the door of the compartment, scratching his head confusedly, wondering who I was.

9
SPECIAL TASK FORCE AND THE KILLING OF SRIPRAKASH SHUKLA

It all started in Gorakhpur—the city named after the ascetic saint Gorakhnath but now known as the home ground of Yogi Adityanath, the present-day CM of Uttar Pradesh. The birthplace of Urdu poet Firaq Gorakhpuri, Sant Kabir Das and freedom fighter Ram Prasad Bismil, it is also the place where Munshi Premchand wrote some of his immortal works.

However, as a police officer, I always thought of Gorakhpur as the place that has been the hotbed of some of UP's most dreaded gangsters. In the Seventies and Eighties, the warlords of two gangs—Hari Shankar Tiwari and Vijendra Pratap Shahi—held sway over the region. Between these two gangs, an astonishing number of murders were executed. At that time, Gorakhpur was notorious for gunfights, extortions, kidnappings, smuggling and illegal contracts. Much before Mumbai or even Italy, gang wars had become common in Gorakhpur. The city infamously earned the nicknames Chicago of the East and Slice of Sicily. But this wasn't simply a mafia war. Caste politics was at play too.

Hari Shankar Tiwari came from an affluent family and was a Brahmin by caste. Vijendra Pratap Shahi represented the Thakur lobby. The complex caste equation often seen in the state further galvanized the rivalry between the two. Lack of industrialization and presence of the license-permit-raj worked as a stimulus to their anti-state activities. The dictum of the day was that the one who could take everything by force would rule the city. Thus, lands were illegally occupied, businessmen were terrorized, guns were smuggled, illegal country-made pistols were manufactured in large quantities and the city became a battleground for gang wars. For almost two and a half decades, Hari Shankar Tewari and Vijendra Pratap Shahi headed the dominant gangs of Gorakhpur, until one day when a young man from the same city disrupted this equation. His name was Sriprakash Shukla.

THE DAREDEVIL SHUKLA

Sriprakash Shukla hailed from an ordinary lower-middle class family. Being the only son of a Brahmin schoolteacher in Gorakhpur's Mamkhor village, he was pampered, even though his family had limited means. Even as a boy, Shukla

Biting the Bullet

had an inordinate fondness for what these days is termed as 'good life'. He loved good food and bodybuilding. Soon, he joined the local *akhara* (wrestling ring) and became a wrestler. As the popular young *pehlwaan* (wrestler) of his mohalla, Shukla was admired and idolized by the young boys of his locality. All was well in Shukla's world until a boy called Rakesh Tiwari teased his sister on the road.

Rakesh Tiwari was a mere ruffian, a testosterone-driven young man, for whom teasing and wolf-whistling at hapless girls on the road was but a matter of daily routine. This time, however, his act of harassment would change the course of crime in Uttar Pradesh.

When Rakesh Tiwari whistled at Shukla's sister, the latter flew into a rage. He caught hold of Tiwari and kept beating him till he died on the spot! The sister was shocked and so was the entire city, especially his family members. Shukla fled to Bangkok to escape arrest, and thus began the journey of a dreaded gangster. Years later, when Shukla returned from Bangkok, he had already decided his career path. He had tasted blood. He did not want to return to his modest means of existence. But he needed someone to help him enter the world of crime. Help arrived in the form of Suraj Bhan.

A dreaded mafia don who ruled northern Bihar, eastern Uttar Pradesh and areas of Nepal, Suraj Bhan was a heaven-sent opportunity for Shukla. He dealt in firearms and his name was a terror in the area of his influence. In turn, Shukla impressed Bhan with his energy. In the years ahead, Shukla found the perfect mentor in Bhan. Suraj Bhan had a huge cache of sophisticated arms and Shukla got his hands on a few of them. He gradually befriended men of his own temperament, who were lured by gunpower and quick money. Soon, he had a small gang of his own. He was already wanted on one count of murder. With the blessings of Suraj Bhan, he heralded the beginning of an unprecedented era of crime in Uttar Pradesh.

ANNOUNCING HIS ENTRY WITH A BANG!

The rivalry between Hari Shankar Tiwari and Virendra Pratap Shahi was still dictating UP's crime scene. For Shukla to make his presence felt, he needed to announce his entry with a bang. An opportunity presented itself in 1997.

Virendra Pratap Shahi was a sitting MLA from Lakshmipur in Maharajganj. He had about sixty criminal cases against him and had been nicknamed Sher-e-Purvanchal in the region. It was a usual morning in one of the posh colonies of Lucknow, when all of a sudden, the residents were suddenly disturbed by a series of gunshots. Minutes later, the news of Virendra Shahi's murder was the talking point of the city. And the assassin was none other than Sriprakash Shukla.

The sensational murder sent shockwaves, not only through the administration, but also amongst the mafia. The old order of Hari Shankar Tiwari and Virendra Pratap Shahi was now toppled. The name of Sriprakash Shukla flashed in newspaper headlines on a daily basis, and the young man became a don overnight. The fact that a sitting MLA could be murdered in his home raised a serious question. Could the government of the day be trusted with the safety and security of the common man? Within days, Shukla's persona had assumed devilish proportions.

Hari Shankar Tiwari had represented the Chillupar constituency for more than fifteen years. And Sriprakash now wanted to contest from this constituency. This was a very daring and bold intention and some would even say a bit foolish, but Shukla had made his intentions clear. He wanted to enter politics and establish his supremacy by annihilating the veterans of the region. The mere information of his intention to kill Hari Shankar Tiwari was enough to jolt the administration.

At this juncture, I was posted as the ADG of the PAC in Lucknow. I was not a part of mainstream police administration; I was watching all these developments with great interest from the outside. Around me, people were speculating who Shukla's next target was going to be. One day, while returning to Lucknow from Sitapur, I got the information that Shukla had committed yet another sensational crime. This time it was a multiple murder of three persons in the well-known Dilip Hotel, located close to the UP Vidhan Sabha. Apparently, Shukla, armed with an AK-47, had entered the hotel and shot down three persons. This was the first crime in UP in which an AK-47 had been used. AK-47 is a prohibited weapon, authorized for use only by the army and the police. But these were the times when gangsters were making all-out efforts to arm themselves with the most lethal and sophisticated weapons.

Shukla continued with his series of sensational killings. He gunned down a well-known contractor and his aide. He then killed Brij Bihari Prasad, a minister in Bihar, inside a hospital. Ajit Sircar, another MLA from Bihar, also fell prey to Shukla's bullets. He continued killing important and well known people with impunity. These murders sent the CM and the state administration into a spin. It was high time that Shukla's reign of terror was put to an end. The million-dollar question was, who would bell the cat?

THE PLOT TO ASSASSINATE THE CHIEF MINISTER

Matters came to head when Shukla took a contract of five crore rupees to assassinate Kalyan Singh, the CM of UP at the time. As soon as the CM learnt of this, he summoned the DGP and apprised him of the news. Why was it, he demanded to know, that the intelligence branch had not told him about this? The DGP was also perturbed by this serious intelligence lapse.

One morning, the CM summoned me to his residence immediately. The urgency in the message surprised me. I wondered if it had anything to do with Sriprakash Shukla. I drove straight to the CM's residence in Lucknow from Sitapur. He greeted me with a muted smile. Niceties over, he came straight to the point.

'I have had it with Sriprakash Shukla! He is committing such high profile murders with impunity now, that my government is beginning to seem spineless,' he said. The CM suspected that Shukla's menace had grown beyond

Biting the Bullet

the capabilities of the local police. He asked if I could immediately take over the post of the Additional Director General of Police (Law and Order) and take the responsibility of bringing Shukla to book. He told me that the DGP and he both believed that I was the man for the job.

I was half expecting this but wasn't happy. Having served twice already at this very post, I knew what a heavy toll it wreaked on one's family life. In fact, being quite fed up with the constant stress, I had requested to be placed in my present position in the PAC, a force for whom I had a special affinity. When I said as much to the CM, he was disappointed. That was when he told me about the contract on his life. After hearing the CM's tale of woe, the policeman within me had no alternative but to accept the challenge. But I had a demand of my own.

Kalyan Singh was all ears. Over the years, in many of my postings, I had worked hard to create crack teams for anti-dacoity operations. The need of the hour was to develop an elite force of police personnel, with outstanding capabilities in tracking down criminals and gangs, experienced in shootouts with hardened criminals, good in intelligence gathering and of high integrity. If the CM sanctioned it, this was the perfect opportunity to set up such a force. I told the CM that to achieve success against a gangster like Shukla, such a force was essential.

This force would be called the Special Task Force (STF).

Ajai Raj Sharma

THE CREATION OF THE SPECIAL TASK FORCE

I had been working on a blueprint for the STF long before it had even been agreed upon. It would be created from the existing police force of the state. Keeping in view the nature of the STF and the stress and danger involved in its functioning, I proposed that the members of this unit should be young and physically very fit, all below the age of thirty-five years. They had to be good marksmen, be committed and display impeccable integrity. An officer of the rank of an SSP/SP, who would be assisted by two DSPs, would head the STF. Each member of this force would be entitled to additional pay of 30 per cent.

The idea was approved in record time by the DGP and the home secretary, and I was posted as ADG (Law and Order) with an additional charge of ADG of STF. The only task for this unit was to constantly track Shukla and his gang till they finally got him.

I left the CM's residence feeling like I had taken on a huge responsibility. Shukla was wily and dangerous; bringing him to book would not be easy. The next morning, I met the DGP and informed him about all that had transpired. I requested him to allow me to select and post the personnel required for the STF. At that time, Arun Kumar was posted as the SSP of Lucknow. He was already investigating the murders committed by Shukla and had, therefore, acquired a lot of information about his gang and their modus operandi. He was the obvious choice as the SSP of STF.

Biting the Bullet

Little did I realize then, that the STF would, in later years, be declared a great success and its prototypes created in other states as well.

KEEPERS OF THE LAW IN UP

With my new posting, putting an end to the reign of terror unleashed not only by Sriprakash Shukla, but other mafia dons like Munna Bajrangi and Raju Bhatnagar became my responsibility. Arun Kumar and I lost no time in selecting the best personnel, including the best SIs, head constables and constable drivers for STF. We also simultaneously ordered ten sturdy SUVs. In the first meeting of the STF, I addressed the men.

'All of you who are attending this meeting have been chosen because you are the best. You have been selected to create history, to accomplish something which the UP and Bihar Police have failed to achieve thus far!' I said. 'I have accepted the challenge posed to us by Sriprakash Shukla because I have full faith in all of you and your capabilities.' I asked all those present in the meeting if we would succeed in our mission. As soon as I finished speaking, there was a thunderous response: 'We will, we will!' the men shouted as one. I was happy to see that the personnel selected for the STF indeed had a very high morale.

Without further ado, we divided the men into eight teams, which would target eight gangs in the state. Headed by an inspector, each team would consist of an SI, a head constable, two constables and a constable driver. They would have a fast-moving SUV fitted with state-of-the-art communication systems and all necessary long range and close combat weapons. Each team would track a single gang, study its *modus operandi*, map its known locations and send daily intelligence reports to the STF headquarters.

THE SENSATIONAL KIDNAPPING OF A CHEMIST'S SON

Within two weeks of the formation of the STF, all the chemists in the state went on strike. Shukla had kidnapped Kunal Rastogi, the young son of the influential president of the Pharmaceutical Association of the state. In the scuffle that ensued during the kidnap bid, Shukla fatally shot the senior Rastogi. In protest, all pharmaceutical distributors and retailers went on a blanket strike. Patients were going without medicines; some were getting it at exorbitant prices from the black market, while others were getting spuriously-made medicines. In short, the entire medical ecosystem was in chaos.

Slogans were raised against the inefficiency of Lucknow Police, making the situation also politically sensitive. Shukla's crimes were tarnishing the reputation of the UP Police further and further. The anxiety of the state government was palpable. The opposition parties were leaving no stone unturned to turn this into an embarrassment for the ruling party, and the media, day after day, were publishing stories about the rise of a new don. In short, the state was sitting on a tinderbox.

Biting the Bullet

A NEW ERA IN COMMUNICATION

Seemingly oblivious to the havoc he was wreaking, Shukla was living a flamboyant lifestyle. Mobile phones had just become the new status symbol and Shukla soon lost no time in acquiring one. He would flaunt his mobile phone and boast to his peers that his daily mobile bill was in thousands (an exorbitant amount at that time). As per our sources, he was constantly on the mobile phone with clients (victims) and his girlfriend—or shall we say girlfriends, for Shukla was known for his love for pretty women as much as he was known for his other excesses. Little did he know then that one day his own Motorola phone would prove to be his nemesis.

At STF, we realized that mobile phones could be used to track users, something that had not been possible earlier and others had not thought about. But Shukla was always thinking one step ahead. He would never use the same number for long and would even switch sim cards between calls. It is said that he would use as many as fourteen sim cards simultaneously. This made our task that much harder but at least we could see the road ahead. We kept tracking his calls to see if we could find a pattern. STF officers became regular visitors to telecom companies, learning how to track mobile calls more and more effectively.

One night, we got information that Shukla was in Lucknow. He was spotted near an eating joint. I still remember that it was raining very heavily that night at about 10 p.m. As soon as his car was seen near a rather lonely restaurant, it was given chase by the police patrol car, which was cruising in the vicinity. The patrol car sent a message about the location of Shukla's car to the control room. One of the STF officers also joined the chase.

But Shukla was a master driver. He swerved into a side lane to confuse his pursuers. It was pouring cats and dogs. In the darkness and the rain, the police was finding it hard to track Shukla as he wove in and out of lanes until he ultimately reached a busy highway. In the heavy traffic, the police were being blinded by the headlights of vehicles coming from the opposite direction. The car chase that had begun so dramatically, ended with a whimper. Shukla managed to give a slip to the police cars chasing him. We had missed our target by a whisker!

Needless to say, the press and public lambasted us for allowing Shukla to escape. The CM was particularly unhappy with us. The pressure was mounting even as Shukla's threat was getting more serious by the day.

HIS LAST THREAT

It was September 1998. My phone rang when I was having dinner at home. It was a senior cardiologist at Lucknow's King George Medical College. I had known his family since my days as the SSP of Allahabad. He had treated my mother and was like family to me. He sounded very nervous and insisted on meeting me at that very moment. He came over with an elderly friend, a famous hotelier and builder from the city, who had just received an extortion call from Shukla.

Biting the Bullet

I assured the old gentleman that we would protect him.

My request to him was, 'Whenever you receive the next call from Shukla, please try to prolong the conversation with him.'

The old gentleman protested: 'I don't want to speak with him even for a minute and you are asking me to prolong the conversation. I just told you how abusive and brash he is!' This was, I explained, our best chance of nabbing him. If he prolonged the calls, our officers could track his location.

Shukla called the old man the very next day. With our newly-acquired knowledge of tracking mobile calls, we were both anxious and confident. And as per the decided script, the old man kept on talking and Shukla, from the other side, marshalled the choicest of abuses. We had still not managed to trace the call. My officers kept signaling the old man to keep talking and he obliged us. There was a time when he started weeping because Shukla's language was getting too foul for his quintessential *Lucknowi tehzeeb*, the fabled etiquette of Lucknow. But he controlled himself and kept up the conversation.

The ruse worked. We were able to trace the call to Delhi's Vasant Kunj area. I immediately called and ordered Arun Kumar to take the first available flight to Delhi, along with the concerned STF team. I also called the commissioner of police, Delhi, and informed him that my team was reaching Delhi the same evening to try and nab Shukla. I requested him to nominate an officer, who could be contacted by the STF officers for further action in Delhi. He nominated the ACP of the Special Cell of Delhi Police to coordinate with the officers of STF and give necessary support to them. I, too, took the first flight to Delhi the next morning.

We all knew that Shukla used fourteen sim cards to avoid being detected. However, for reasons we'll never know, in the last seven days of his life, he constantly used only one mobile number. Call it fate or our good fortune, this made our job of tracking him much easier. All we now had to do was to track Shukla's calls and wait to nab him.

An opportunity presented itself the very next day.

Shukla was a bit of a playboy, something that his girlfriend in Gorakhpur naturally didn't like. She called him up, angry and suspicious that he was cheating on her. People heard Shukla pacifying her, saying that he was returning to Gorakhpur by the early morning Indian Airlines flight the next day. This was a piece of golden information for us. We knew the flight and its timings and most importantly, that in the airport Shukla would be unarmed. This was our best chance and we could not let it pass.

22 SEPTEMBER 1998, DELHI AIRPORT, 3.30 A.M.

On the evening of 21 September at about 5 p.m., the Special Cell and the STF personnel had met at the Delhi airport to chalk out a plan to nab Shukla the next morning. Every member of both the units was explained his role in the plan, as well as the specific point where he was supposed to locate himself. On the morning of 22 September, at 3.30 a.m., all were positioned at their allotted points, waiting to jump into action to nab their prized catch.

Biting the Bullet

The flight was scheduled to depart at 5.45 a.m. Passengers began trickling in. A close watch was being kept on every arriving passenger who was being checked in. Boarding was soon announced, but Shukla still had not arrived. The plane to Gorakhpur took off, and Shukla had not turned up, leaving everyone in bewilderment and great disappointment.

How did he know that he was being tracked and that the STF was waiting for him? It was a frustrating mystery for all of us. All we could do was to continue tracking him and wait for another opportune moment.

We intercepted another call from Shukla to his girlfriend in Gorakhpur again, apologizing that he couldn't make the flight as he had unfinished business in Ghaziabad. Our officers listened intently as Shukla told his girlfriend that he'd reach Ghaziabad around 2 p.m., finish his work and take the next morning's flight to Gorakhpur.

We rushed to Ghaziabad and put up camouflaged pickets along his route. Our plan was to surround him as soon as an opportunity presented itself. We did not want to wait for another day.

Shukla had some eccentric habits. One of them, which I must mention here, was that he was a compulsive car thief. I am using the word 'compulsive' here with a purpose. He was so crazy about cars that whenever he took a fancy to one, he would steal it! This made tracking him a problem, for he was forever changing cars. Around this time, Daewoo Motors of Korea came up with a model called Cielo, and it caught the attention of the car-crazy rich upper class. Shukla, too, was enamoured by a blue-coloured Cielo. He lifted it from one of the important markets of south Delhi. Amongst the hidden world of crime and informants, it came to be known that Shukla travelled in a blue-coloured Cielo. This became his biggest giveaway.

One team of Delhi Police was deployed around his hideout in Vasant Kunj to watch his movements. The team was specifically told to only follow him and not to make any move, should it alert the man. He was a trigger-happy criminal and would not have thought twice before shooting even in a residential area.

Till noon there was no movement.

Meanwhile, the STF was deployed at all the crucial junctures on the way from Delhi to Ghaziabad. Special teams were formed to keep an eye on his movements. The trap was laid in time for the return journey. There were five car-borne police teams near the Mohan Nagar flyover on National Highway 24 at 1.50 p.m.

Shukla's favourite, the blue-coloured Cielo had a fake number, HR-26G73, which had been actually allotted to a scooter. It was spotted zooming at great speed on NH-24 in Ghaziabad, after having navigated the congested traffic in Delhi. Shukla was at the wheel, along with his accomplices Anuj Pratap Singh in the passenger seat and Sudhir Tripathi in the back seat. Anuj Pratap Singh was, in fact, the son of a police inspector. When I had come to know of this fact, I had summoned that Inspector but he had completely denied this. I had told him that sometimes young people do get influenced by the wrong people. If he became our informer, I could protect him. But the Inspector continued to stubbornly deny his son's involvement with Shukla. And now, this same Anuj Pratap Singh was accompanying Shukla on what would prove to be their last drive together.

Somehow, Shukla sensed that something was not right. The Cielo suddenly picked up pace. A police gypsy tried to come in its way but he swiftly dodged it. He was so fast that he managed to get past another police gypsy. A third police gypsy driven by SI V.P.S. Chauhan blocked the road. Shukla had nowhere to run.

HIS LAST RUN

With so many criminal cases against him, it seemed like Shukla was forever running away from the law. This was his chance to surrender and let the law take its course. He had also planned to quit active crime and join politics, which, as they say, is a safe haven for criminals. But the young don wanted to better himself against the police; he detested the force and the law of the land, and to him, to surrender would have been too meek.

Instead, he drove off the road and on to an unpaved path. This was the monsoon season and there were potholes and slush on this unmetalled road. On either side were waterlogged fields. The wheels of his car became stuck.

The STF was anticipating the worst and they were not wrong. Shukla started firing indiscriminately at the policemen. His associates also joined him in firing and attacking the police. It was the last desperate attempt of Shukla and his gang to break through police pickets. But they were up against the STF. And the STF was a determined lot.

The STF men retaliated with all their might, with nearly three times the firepower of the gangsters. Within minutes, the biggest gangster of his time, the man who had taken on a contract to kill the CM, the mafia don who considered himself to be invincible, was lying in a pool of blood, dead. His accomplices were also killed along with him.

He was only twenty-five years old.

10

MY DAYS WITH DELHI POLICE

On 29 June 1999, I received a phone call that changed my journey in the police forever. I was sitting in my office in the Border Security Force (BSF) headquarters, when I received a call from the home secretary, government of India. He informed me that orders for my posting as commissioner of police, Delhi, were being issued. I was flabbergasted: it had been barely six months since I had joined the BSF as the additional director general. Also, officers of other state cadres were very rarely posted as commissioner of police, Delhi.

I was, frankly unprepared for the sudden transfer. At that time, the Indo-Pak war was in progress in Kargil. It was not an appropriate time to be transferred from the BSF. I appealed to the then Home Minister L.K. Advani to revoke my orders. The Director General, BSF, also supported my representation. Despite my arguments, the request was turned down. I was asked to join my new post immediately.

Besides the disturbance in my career progression, this posting order made me feel very uncomfortable. This was because I had been asked to replace my batchmate and friend V.N. Singh, who was the commissioner of police at that time. In November 1998, the Delhi state assembly elections were held. The Congress Party had won the elections on two major points—steep rise of onion prices and unsatisfactory state of law and order in Delhi. Unfortunately, in the last few months before I joined as CP Delhi, some sensational cases of murders such as those of Jessica Lal, Irfan Hussain and Shivani Bhatnagar had taken place in Delhi, which had brought a lot of adverse publicity to Delhi Police. I anticipated that due to this, V.N. Singh, who was a fine and upright officer, was not allowed to complete his tenure and transferred prematurely. Since my representation against my transfer order was turned down, I had no choice but to join the new post on 1 July 1999.

En route to the Delhi Police headquarters that day, I remember feeling acutely nervous. I had never served in Delhi Police before. I didn't know the men I had to command. And I had no idea about how to police Delhi!

This could well turn out to be my Waterloo...

Within hours of taking charge, I had to address my first press conference.

Biting the Bullet

THE FIRST PRESS CONFERENCE

Lights flashed and cameras turned towards me. Members of the print and electronic media were waiting eagerly for me. It seemed to me that they were already eager to draw blood. A well-known journalist said that I had arrived in Delhi with a reputation for being able to handle crime with a firm hand. He asked me how I proposed to handle the prevailing deteriorating crime situation in Delhi. Regardless of my nerves, I certainly was not going to be taken to town by this guy. I replied that I did not have any magic wand with which I could just wish away the crime prevailing in Delhi, but would certainly make my best efforts to control the prevalent crime to the extent possible. The media should not expect a crimeless Delhi under my tenure as this was impossible and was only a Utopian idea.

Another journalist told me that in Lucknow, due to the successes I had achieved in quelling notorious gangsters, I had been nicknamed by the press as 'Dirty Harry'. He went on to inform me that sometime back an unfortunate incident had taken place in which an innocent person had been shot dead due to mistaken identity. An assistant commissioner of police had led the police party involved in this incident. The entire police party was arrested and all the policemen involved were sent to jail. The journalist continued to inform me that ever since then, the entire Delhi Police had become totally demoralized. They had become very hesitant to use firearms even when confronting armed gangsters and terrorists. His question was how I proposed to re-energize the force. The police should never be trigger-happy, I replied. I would view fake encounters very adversely. However, like all citizens, policemen also had the right to defend themselves and I would expect them not to hesitate to use this right when necessary.

Having been used only to the ways of the media in UP, this experience made me realize the enormity of the task that lay ahead. For my arena was no longer some districts of UP that few knew or cared about, but the capital of the nation, where every crime made it to the front page of the mainstream media. Every mistake I made would be similarly highlighted, I imagined. However, for a hardened cop like me, there was no option but to soldier on...

TWO SHOOTOUTS SET THE PACE...

Within a few days of my assuming charge, the first challenge presented itself. We received information that a group of notorious gangsters from Meerut led by the notorious Siriya Pehelwaan and Madan Bhaiya (a politician with a reputation of being a criminal) were in town. They had assembled in the well-known Ashok Hotel reportedly to collect *firauti* (ransom money), from a businessman they had kidnapped from Meerut. On getting this information, a crime branch team reached the hotel. A daylight shootout took place outside the hotel in which Siriya Pehelwaan was killed and Madan Bhaiya, along with other members of the gang, was arrested in possession of sophisticated weapons. This was a significant success for my team and it not only helped to raise the morale of the force but brought a lot of appreciation for the performance of the Delhi Police.

Close on the heels of this incident, yet another shootout took place. This time it was between a police patrol party and robbers who were attempting to escape after looting several lakhs of rupees from a businessman. As a result of this shootout, the entire looted money was recovered. Both these incidents were god sent for me. They not only helped to send a message that the Delhi Police now meant serious business but also helped to leash the activities of criminals.

As a result, newspapers started bringing out stories of our success on the front pages instead of the news of murders being committed. This gave the image of Delhi Police a much-needed boost and instilled a sense of security amongst the citizens of the national capital.

AN OUTSIDER LOOKING IN

As things settled down, I followed the protocol that had always stood me in good stead at the district level—I visited every police station in Delhi to meet as many officers and men of the force as possible. As an outsider, I wanted to know first-hand the problems that were bothering them and were responsible for their low morale. There had been some resentment when an out-of-state officer had been appointed as the commissioner and I was keen to build a rapport with my team of officers across the city.

The Delhi Police personnel had three major grievances. The first was the stoppage of the dearness allowance portion of the thirteenth month's salary. The Delhi Police personnel have had the unique privilege of being sanctioned thirteen months' salary in a year, compared to other state police forces who get paid only for twelve months. A few years ago, the dearness allowance of the extra month's salary had been revoked. Many of my predecessors had tried to restore this payment but had failed.

The force was also disgruntled because their casual leave had been curtailed from fifteen to eight days. Its third grievance was that the senior head constables, who had got their last promotion about sixteen years back, had no hope of getting any further promotions. Many head constables told me that they were not motivated to work, as they knew that they would retire at the rank they had already attained.

It was clear that these grievances had to be redressed as soon as possible to raise the morale of the Delhi Police and enhance its performance. Even though I was met with strong resistance, I was able to convince the government about the genuineness of all the three issues.

Consequently, the payment of the dearness allowance of the thirteenth month's salary was allowed, the curtailed casual leave of Delhi Police personnel was restored to fifteen days and above all, 1,100 new posts of assistant sub-inspectors were created, which eased the blockage of promotions for the head constables. Needless to mention, these sanctions brought a lot of joy to the force, and as a result, their high morale became very evident from their future performances.

Biting the Bullet

This also helped me to break the ice with Delhi Police. I was no longer an outsider.

My staff officer, DCP Shankar Dash, played a very significant role in the early stage of my tenure. A highly intelligent and dependable officer, Shankar possessed an excellent knowledge of Delhi, as well as of the officers and men of the Delhi Police, which, for me, proved invaluable on many an occasion. He was always by my side, helping me to tackle one tricky situation after another. During this period, many in Delhi Police were sure that I would not be able to last long, mainly because I was ignorant about the complications involved in administering Delhi and handling Delhi Police itself. With Shankar assisting me, navigating the tricky waters of the capital became that much easier. I will always be indebted to him for his help and assistance.

THE CRICKET MATCH-FIXING CASE

As 1999 drew to a close, one of the most sensational cases of my tenure occurred. A businessman from the busy Karol Bagh area complained that he was receiving frequent calls from some person who was demanding fifty lakh rupees from him. The Delhi Police immediately tapped his phones. It turned out that these calls were being initiated from Dubai by a shadowy underworld figure, Shaheen Hatheli. This case was simple. However, our wiretaps revealed something interesting.

Apparently, some punters in India, in connivance with Dubai's underworld, had been contacting members of the

South African cricket team then playing a series of one-day matches against the Indian team. These surreptitious calls were being made to 'fix' the ongoing matches in lieu of large amounts of money. At the heart of our discovery was a man named Sanjeev Chawla. He had been seen visiting Hansie Cronje, the captain of the South African team, in his room at Hotel Taj Palace in Delhi. Through another wiretap, we learnt that a promised amount had been deposited in Cronje's account in a bank in London.

Baffled but intrigued by this unprecedented situation, I called a meeting of the officials of the Crime Branch and some legal luminaries. The entire dimensions of this case were examined in depth. We read and reread the transcripts of all these conversations. After this matter had been examined from every point of view, the Crime Branch was of the opinion that a case of cheating the public at large was clear and an FIR should be registered. As I am myself a lover of cricket and, as Hansie Cronje had been one of my cricketing idols, I agreed to the proposal with a very heavy heart.

Since this issue involved a foreign nation with whom our country enjoyed friendly and cordial relations, the matter was extremely sensitive and required to be handled with great care and foresight. All the facts were brought to the knowledge of the lieutenant governor of Delhi, the foreign minister and the home secretary. The home minister at that time was out of Delhi and so was the prime minister. When the prime minister returned, the high commissioner of South Africa showed her great resentment and protested

Biting the Bullet

that a case had been registered against the captain and some of the other members of the South African team, who were celebrities and had a great fan following in South Africa. This naturally was very disturbing for the prime minister, who, in turn, spoke to the home minister and expressed his great displeasure about the decision of the Delhi Police to register a case against the members of the South African team.

The home minister summoned the lieutenant governor and me to his office the next day. On the way, something fortuitous happened. A South African journalist called me to ask about my reaction to the confession made by Hansie Cronje hardly an hour ago! The journalist told me that Hansie Cronje had confessed that he and some of his teammates had cheated and indulged in match-fixing for monetary gains. He had made this confession in a church before a priest.

After hearing this news, I felt very relieved and happy as our stand had been vindicated. When the home minister asked me why a criminal case was registered against members of the South African team, I requested him to allow me to switch on the television in his office. As soon as I switched on the TV, the home minister witnessed Hansie Cronje kneeling on his knees before a priest, and making his confession. I didn't need to explain any more.

A lot of effort was made to interrogate Sanjeev Chawla, Hansie Cronje and the other members of the team involved in the match-fixing. However, efforts made via the foreign ministry and through the Interpol were not successful.

Without being able to interrogate the key players, the Delhi Police investigation could not progress further. A non-bailable warrant issued against Sanjeev Chawla by the court was sent to the UK for execution through Interpol, which also issued a Red Corner Notice against him. However, no reply to the letter rogatory sent to the UK and South Africa was received during my remaining tenure as CP Delhi.

The match-fixing case unearthed by the Delhi Police was indeed unique. The effort put into exposing the entire scandal was highly praiseworthy. Prior to this case, match-fixing in the world of cricket was unheard-of and was beyond the common man's imagination. This spectacular success brought great appreciation for the Delhi Police internationally.

THE RED FORT TERRORIST ATTACK

On 22 December 2000, we received the most unexpected and perturbing information late in the evening. Six persons in dark clothes and armed with AK-47 weapons had entered the Red Fort, in which an army unit was stationed. Inside the Fort, the group fired at a sentry, killing him on the spot. Thereafter, they continued to run across the complex and shot at a soldier, seriously injuring him. Sensing serious danger from the intruders, the unit's quick reaction team (QRT) returned fire. However, the intruders, taking advantage of the cover of darkness, escaped into the nearby woods. Who could have imagined that a terrorist group would have the guts to attack a place as important as the

Red Fort, which was guarded by an army unit?

I was on leave when this happened. On getting this information, R.K. Sharma, the special commissioner, who in my absence, was the officiating CP Delhi, rushed to the spot with other police officers. They were initially not allowed entry into the Fort by army personnel, who stated that they were themselves looking into the matter. However, when the police explained to them the legal position and told them that the police were duty-bound to register a case and take up its investigation, they were allowed entrance. Thereafter, the investigation started in right earnest.

Initially, neither did anybody have a clue about the identity of the intruders nor did anybody know why they had attacked the Red Fort. Several theories about the attack began doing the rounds. The crime team, photographers and dog squad were all pressed into action. The investigation of the case was handed over to the Special Cell of the Delhi Police, who, in tandem with central intelligence agencies, tried to figure out the identity of these intruders. Early next morning, all the area adjacent to the Red Fort was thoroughly combed. A nondescript piece of paper was found on which a mobile number had been scribbled. This was a very lucky break and ultimately gave the investigation the right direction.

The phone number was traced to a Delhi Development Authority apartment complex in Ghazipur. On 25 December, the police raided the apartments and apprehended one Ashfaq Ahmed, alias Abu Hammad alias Arif Mohammad. He belonged to Abbottabad in Pakistan and was from the terror outfit Lashkar-e-Taiba (LeT). Ahmed had married an Indian national, Rehana, who was living with him in the DDA flat. He was found in possession of a pistol and a fake ration card. Rehana was also subsequently arrested.

Preliminary enquiries revealed that Ashfaq had been sent to Delhi in May 2000 on the directions of Pakistan's ISI. He had been entrusted with the job of setting up a safe and camouflaged base, in a suitable area in Delhi for carrying out subversive activities. He accordingly set up a computer centre known as 'Knowledge Plus' in Jamia Nagar. The ISI gave him full support and provided him substantial money for carrying out the task entrusted to him. His Indian wife, Rehana, had full knowledge of the activities of her husband.

Further interrogations revealed that Ashfaq had settled down in Delhi for carrying out terrorist attacks. He had regular consultations with his handlers across the border. Subsequently, five militants, namely, Abu Samal, Abu Saad, Abu Shukhar, Bilal Ahmed and Haider joined him to carry out nefarious plans. In due course of time, Ashfaq hired an accommodation in Batla House, located in Jamia Nagar, south Delhi. This accommodation was to serve as a hideout for visiting militants. He also planned and arranged necessary transport and communication facilities for the operations to be conducted by the visiting terrorists.

On the fateful day, Ashfaq, with his associate terrorists, reconnoitred the Red Fort area. He, along with other accomplices, gained entry into the Red Fort on the pretext of watching the Light and Sound Show scheduled from 7.30 p.m. to 8.30 p.m. They camouflaged weapons and grenades

Biting the Bullet

on their bodies. After the show, taking advantage of the darkness, Abu Samal and Abu Saad sneaked into the military area with their weapons. The others exited the Red Fort and took positions around the Fort. Two militants who had got inside the Red Fort opened fire at three places, killing three persons, and escaped by coming down the eastern wall of the Red Fort. They dumped their weapons, grenades and ammunitions at a safe place and made good their escape.

During further interrogation, Ashfaq revealed that four of the terrorists had already escaped from Delhi after completing the task and only one of them, Abu Samal, was still staying at Batla House. On this information, on 26 December, a police team went to Batla House and knocked on the door. They were greeted by a burst of fire from inside. The police party retaliated and returned fire. This exchange of fire resulted in the death of Abu Samal. One AK-56 rifle, two magazines and some ammunition were recovered from the spot.

In due course of this investigation, some others were arrested for their role in this conspiracy. The other terrorists who had escaped after the incident from Delhi were declared proclaimed offenders. The case was successfully prosecuted and Ashfaq Ahmed was punished with death sentence, three of the accused were given life imprisonment and some others were punished with seven years' imprisonment.

The successful working out of the Red Fort case in a short time, not only brought a great sense of relief to all of us but also afforded us great satisfaction. Such occasions, which are rare, always bring joy and lessen the stress under which policemen often live. Since the killings in the Red Fort had created a lot of sensation, its successful detection brought about commensurate praise and appreciation for the Delhi Police. It was a landmark achievement for the officers of the Special Cell. As a leader of the force, it was a matter of great pride for me that this superb investigation happened in my absence. R.K. Sharma indeed performed creditably.

THE SENSATIONAL MURDER OF PHOOLAN DEVI

On 25 July 2001, a sensational crime took place in the jurisdiction of the New Delhi district. Phoolan Devi, the erstwhile Bandit Queen and then a Member of Parliament, was shot dead outside her official residence. The murder had taken place when she was disembarking from her car after attending a session in the Parliament. Her assailants had shot her from a very close range, abandoned their green Fiat car and disappeared immediately from the scene.

I got the news of this heinous crime when I was in office. I immediately rushed to the scene of crime and from there to the hospital where she had been taken. While on my way, I gave necessary instructions to the police officers on the spot and issued orders for the crime branch to take over the investigation of the case.

I had barely returned to my office when I received a call from Hardwar. I did not know the caller, but he said that he had known of me since my days in UP. Having seen the TV reports about Phoolan Devi's murder, he was keen to pass on some vital information, which could help to solve the case. It turned out that the green Fiat car used by the killers was owned by one Sher Singh, who was an excise contractor and had a liquor shop in Saharanpur. The informant claimed to know Sher Singh, who he said had reported this car stolen a few months ago. He had even registered an FIR for the theft in Kotwali Dehradun.

This was a lucky break. I directed K.K. Paul, who was heading the Crime Branch at that time, to verify this information. Everything the informant had said to me was ultimately proven correct. Sher Singh became the prime suspect in this murder. He regarded Phoolan Devi as the biggest enemy of the Thakur community, because she had committed a mass murder of some Thakurs in Behmai some years back. To avenge that murder, he decided to kill Phoolan Devi. On 27 July, Sher Singh appeared at the Press Club, Dehradun, and declared before the media that he, along with Rajender Singh, had murdered Phoolan Devi. He was arrested the next day in Saharanpur, while they were trying to surrender in court. They were ultimately convicted.

Though the murder of a Member of Parliament had created a lot of sensation, the swiftness with which the culprits were apprehended and the mystery of the murder solved brought a lot of praise for the Delhi Police. It proved to be yet another feather in their cap.

THE ATTACK ON THE PARLIAMENT

Before the year 2001 came to an end, an unprecedented crime took place, which shook the nation and showed the world the extent to which terrorism had grown. On 13 December, I received a call. Something unthinkable had happened. Terrorists had entered the Parliament premises and were firing incessantly. I had barely kept the phone down, when the control room also confirmed that firing was taking place in the Parliament premises. There was no time to think and plan. I ran out of my office and headed straight to the Parliament. On my way, I called the control room and directed it to ensure that a couple of armed companies reached the Parliament immediately. I also issued orders to certain select officers, particularly those of the Special Cell, to reach the scene of the shootout.

The situation was dire. As the Parliament was in session, the prime minister, along with all the members of his cabinet and the members of the Parliament, were present in the House. I did not even want to imagine the colossal damage the terrorists could potentially cause.

As I was approaching the Parliament, I could still hear some shots being fired. When I reached the scene, a number of dead bodies of terrorists, civilians and the police alike, lay scattered at different places in the complex. I also observed that near the dead bodies of the terrorists, weapons like AK-47 rifles, 9 mm pistols and grenades were scattered. Their mobile phones, which were to provide us valuable information, were there too. I deputed a senior officer to take charge of the scene of crime and ensure that all evidence and clues available at the scene were preserved. Immediately, a cordon was thrown around the area and a very close inspection of everything available on the spot was carried out. I entrusted Rajbir Singh, the ACP of the Special Cell, to at once take over the investigation of the case and report the progress to me by evening.

Thereafter, I went inside the Parliament and met the home minister, who was present with the Speaker of the House in his chamber. Both appeared to be in a state of shock. I assured them that within a couple of days, we would be able to trace the culprits and find out who was behind this incident. We requested all members of Parliament to leave for their respective residences and helped them with necessary transport. Once the Parliament had been vacated, to ensure that no terrorist remained in hiding on the premises, an intensive combing of the Parliament building and its surrounding area was organized.

The next two days were stressful, to say the least. We were besieged by calls from the press asking all sorts of questions about the investigation of the case. The Special Cell team and the central intelligence agencies jointly launched an intensive investigation into the whole incident.

The sim cards of the mobiles of the terrorists contained valuable information and helped to kickstart the investigation. On the basis of the information obtained from these mobiles, four associates of the slain terrorists, namely Mohammad Afzal, Shaukat Hussain Guru, Syed Abdul Rehman Gilani and Navjot Sandhu, wife of Shaukat Hussain Guru, all belonging to Jaish-e-Mohammed (JeM), were arrested. A large number of explosives and incriminating materials were recovered from their possessions. The first three belonged to Jammu and Kashmir. Mohammad Afzal in his interrogation disclosed that he had crossed over to Pakistan and had undergone two and a half months of training at a training camp in PoK, which was run by the Pak ISI. After completing his training, the handlers infiltrated him back to India.

Investigations revealed that the terrorists who had been killed had local support. Syed Abdul Rehman Gilani, a lecturer of Arabic in Zakir Hussain College, had been in touch with them. He, along with Mohammad Afzal and Shaukat Hussain Guru, had been making necessary arrangements for them in Delhi. It emerged that Mohammad Afzal had been very active and was the main coordinator of JeM in Delhi. He further stated that in the first week of December, a meeting had taken place in the house of Shaukat, in which Shaukat Hussain and Mohammad Afzal were present along with the terrorists. In this meeting, they discussed a plan to carry out an attack on the Parliament House.

After her arrest, Navjot Sandhu disclosed that after the incident of 13 December 2001, Shaukat Hussain and Mohammad Afzal had immediately left in a truck for Srinagar. This information was given to J&K Police, who located the truck and apprehended both Mohammad Afzal and Shaukat Hussain. A laptop and ten lakh rupees were recovered from their possession.

On being subjected to intensive interrogation, Mohammad Afzal disclosed that he used to visit Delhi for business purposes regularly. In February 2001, he was contacted by Tariq, a close associate of Ghazi Baba, a

Biting the Bullet

Pakistani national, who was the supreme commander of JeM in India. According to him, Tariq motivated him to join JeM. He took him to Ghazi Baba, who had his base in Abu Hills, Pahalgam. Ghazi Baba informed Mohammad Afzal that under pressure from the ISI chief, both Masood Azhar of JeM and Zaki-ur-Rehman Lakhvi of LeT had joined forces. The Pak ISI had issued directions to them, to carry out a *fidayeen* attack in Delhi. Ghazi Baba directed Mohammad Afzal to go back to Delhi and set up a base. Consequently, Mohammad Afzal came to Delhi. He motivated Shaukat Hussain and Syed Abdul Rehman Gilani to be a part of the conspiracy for conducting the *fidayeen* attack.

In the month of October 2001, Ghazi Baba introduced Mohammad Afzal to another JeM militant. His name was Mohammad. He was also a Pak national. Mohammad Afzal was informed that Mohammad would lead the proposed *fidayeen* attack in Delhi. Thus, Mohammad Afzal brought Mohammad to Delhi and arranged a safe hideout for him in Mukherjee Nagar. Leaving Mohammad at the hideout, Mohammad Afzal, after a week, returned to Srinagar. Shaukat Hussain arranged another safe hideout in Gandhi Vihar. On returning to Srinagar, Mohammad Afzal met Tariq again. Tariq introduced Mohammad Afzal to yet another two JeM militants, Raja and Haider, both of whom were Pakistani nationals. In November 2001, Afzal brought them to Delhi and took them to the hideout in Gandhi Vihar. After a week, Mohammad Afzal returned to Srinagar and met Tariq again. He was introduced by Tariq to two more militants—another Raja and Hamza (both Pakistani). They were brought to Delhi in the beginning of the first week of December 2001. They brought with them AK rifles, pistols, a grenade launcher, grenades, detonators, radioactive devices and wireless sets—hidden in their baggage.

In order to reconnoitre the Parliament House area, Afzal purchased a black Yamaha motorcycle. The Parliament House and the surrounding areas were reconnoitred several times. They also purchased five mobile phones and some police uniforms. They prepared fake ID cards and a parking sticker for their vehicle for entering the Parliament premises. On 11 December, they purchased a second-hand white ambassador car from Karol Bagh. They fitted this car with tinted glass and a red light. The seller of this car had identified it when visuals of the car were displayed by news channels after the attack. This particular seller knew one of the Delhi police officers and informed him about the sale of this car on the date of the incident. The same was conveyed to one of the ACPs and that was how the information reached me. But by that time the incident had already taken place.

On 13 December, all of them met in Gandhi Vihar. Mohammad, the leader of the *fidayeen* group, handed over a laptop and ten lakh rupees to Afzal Guru. He told him that in case they were killed in their mission, the laptop should be handed over to Ghazi Baba and the money should be kept with Afzal for their future expenses. Heavily armed, all five militants then left for the Parliament in the car they had purchased. It is indeed surprising how easily they entered the Parliament campus, by hoodwinking the Watch and Ward staff of the Parliament. Once inside the campus, the militants drove fast, anxious to achieve their mission. Unfortunately, they drove onto a wrong road at the end of which a huge iron gate was chained and locked permanently. Realizing their mistake, they became nervous. They tried to reverse at high speed, but in the process banged against the escort vehicle in the motorcade of the vice president of India. The security persons sitting in the escort vehicle jumped out and tried to stop the ambassador. This resulted in a shootout between them. Unfortunately, the securitymen were at a severe disadvantage, as they were equipped with only close-quarter battle weapons, mostly 9 mm pistols. On the other hand, the militants were using AK-47 rifles. Fortunately, the periphery of the compound was being guarded by a company of the Central Reserve Police Force. On witnessing the shootout inside the campus, they began firing with long-range rifles. The security men fought bravely but four of them fell to the bullets of the militants. Five terrorists, all Pakistani nationals, were also killed in this fierce shootout. Besides them, one unfortunate lady constable of the CRPF, two Watch and Ward men on the rolls of the Parliament and an innocent gardener were also killed. Four security men lost their lives, but they not only saved the day for us but also helped the government from a lot of embarrassment and humiliation. A big service was done by the staff of the Parliament House, when they quickly closed the big wooden doors leading into the Parliament. Even today, when I think about this incident, I shudder to think of the consequences, especially its international ramifications, had the terrorists succeeded in their mission.

Ajai Raj Sharma

ACKNOWLEDGING CROSS-BORDER TERRORISM

The investigation of this case clearly brought out all the facts of this conspiracy. It was evident that the attack had been planned from across the border. I called for a press conference and provided all the details about this *fidayeen* attack and Pakistan's indisputable involvement.

The investigation into the Parliament attack case had far-reaching consequences. For the past several years, the government of India had been telling the US, the UK and other countries that Pakistan was involved in terrorist attacks taking place in India. Unfortunately, these countries did not take the issue of Pakistan's role in the ongoing cross-border terrorism very seriously. However, the facts established by the investigation of this particular case were so convincing that diplomats such as the US Ambassador and the UK High Commissioner in India, were left with no iota of doubt about the role of Pakistan in this condemnable episode. Once they were convinced, the attitude of their respective governments towards Pakistan also underwent a sea change.

The US pressurized General Musharraf and his government to take immediate steps to put an end to the patronage and support being given to militant groups operating from Pakistan soil. The speeches and utterances of General Musharraf in the subsequent months were ample proof of the pressure exerted by the US on Pakistan. General Musharraf, in his address to Pakistan, said that he would not tolerate the soil of his country being used by terrorist groups and warned the ISI for promoting them. The investigation of this case was completed in a record time of six months and was put up for a judicial trial. The main accused was awarded death penalty and some others life sentences. It may be worth mentioning that this was the first case under the Prevention of Terrorist Activities Act (POTA), where the accused were convicted after a very fast trial.

By the end of 2001, I had completed two and a half years of my tenure in Delhi. The tension involved in the job had started taking its toll. I felt the need for a change. I requested the government to consider my transfer. Fortunately for me, my batchmate, who was the then director general of the BSF, was due to retire shortly. The government was kind enough to post me in his vacant position. On 1 July 2002, I handed over the charge of CP, Delhi, after completing a full tenure of three years, a very satisfied man.

When I had joined Delhi Police, I was regarded as an 'outsider'. When I left, I like to think that I had been accepted as one of them by the entire force. When I reminisce about the days I spent with Delhi Police, fond memories come rushing to my mind, especially those in which in the beginning we seemed to be at the receiving end but ultimately we were able to turn into great success stories. There is no doubt in my mind that during my tenure as the commissioner of police, Delhi, god was especially kind to me.

11

THE VALIANT AND VERSATILE BORDER SECURITY FORCE

India shares 3,323 km of its border with Pakistan, stretching from Kutch in Gujarat, Rajasthan and Punjab, all the way to Jammu and Kashmir. On its eastern side, it shares a 4,095-km-long border with Bangladesh. The sentinels of these borders belong to the world's largest border-guarding force, the Border Security Force—BSF.

Until the creation of the BSF, each state had been guarding its frontiers with their own state police armed battalions. The limitations of these state battalions were soon exposed when they were unable to cope with the recurring border violations. Soon after the Chinese and Pakistani aggressions in the early Sixties, a decision was taken to create a strong, unified and organized paramilitary force, under the central government. Hence, the BSF was born on 1 December 1965, under the inspiring leadership of K.F. Rustamji. It began with a total of twenty-five battalions; today the force has grown to 192 battalions and has become the world's largest border guarding force.

When I first joined the BSF as additional director general, I marvelled at the variety of the terrain the force had to operate in. During my six-month stint, I covered a lot of border areas. Whenever I got the chance, I would requisition a helicopter and visit several border outposts in a day. The terrains of the borders are entirely different. In the west, Kutch is all salt and marsh, in Rajasthan there is a desert. In the north, the border in Punjab has thick and tall grass. Jammu and Kashmir is forested and mountainous. On the eastern side, the border with Bangladesh has very thick forests and marshes. The border men, I soon realized, braved raging blizzards, blinding sandstorms and shallow marshes. In fact, having toured all of India's borders extensively, I can say that they have only one trait in common—none of them are easy to navigate.

What is more, when BSF was conceived, it was supposed to manage the security of the borders and matters relating to it. During peace time, it was supposed to promote a sense of security amongst the people residing in the border areas. However, over the years, cross-border crimes—terrorism, smuggling of arms and explosives, narcotics and infiltration have become huge problems, threatening national security. I wondered how one single force could address such a variety of issues, spread over such wide and diverse terrains.

Ajai Raj Sharma

MANAGING THE COUNTRY'S BORDERS

Since the 1971 Indo-Pak War, the very concept of border management has changed. India's borders have traditionally been porous and over the years, several illegal activities like trafficking of arms and drugs, infiltration of anti-national elements and worse, have made border management difficult. At the same time, some of the countries bordering the northeastern states have become safe havens for insurgents in India. It was under these circumstances that securing the entire border with Pakistan as well as Bangladesh was seen as a necessity. The government created a separate department of border management in the ministry of home affairs. It also decided that 3,323 km of our western border with Pakistan and 4,095 km of our eastern border with Bangladesh should be fenced. The BSF was tasked with the fencing of the western borders.

One of the biggest difficulties the BSF faces in handling international borders is that often, the geo-political border does not necessarily resonate with people's hearts. The demarcation of the boundary, especially between India and Bangladesh by Sir Cyril Radcliffe, has been done with complete disregard to human, ethnic and geographical factors. I am tempted to narrate a story in this regard. A senior BSF officer visited a border outpost on the Bangladesh border. He found a person present there, who was not from the BSF. When the officer enquired about him, the visiting officer was informed that this man had been caught several times for border transgressions. I asked him why he crosses the border so frequently. He told me that he had no alternative. He had two wives. They lived on either side of the border and he could not neglect either of them! In West Bengal, there are more than hundred villages located on the zero line. I saw many homes, which have their front door opening into India and the rear one into Bangladesh! This has led to increased border crossings and trans-border crimes. Since the population living on either side of the border is mostly poor, they are tempted to commit crime, primarily on account of their economic needs. Militarily, Bangladesh does not pose a threat to India. However, its borders with India are being used for trafficking arms, drugs and humans, while its border villages are a safe haven for Indian insurgents and Islamic *jihadi*s. This poses a great threat to India's internal security.

Securing the country's western borders has been a greater challenge. The Pakistanis did not want this frontier to be fenced and would fire at the construction workers incessantly. This scared the Public Works Department (PWD) men and their officials who refused to carry on with the job. The Army was also not ready for this task. Hence, the BSF was asked to fence this border. The IG of BSF Jammu Frontier distributed this task between seven battalions. As soon as the BSF deployed bulldozers and excavators on the border and started the job, heavy firing was unleashed from the Pakistani side on the BSF personnel. They would specially target the lights at night, in order to paralyze the ongoing work in the darkness.

One head constable driving an excavator was hit in his

leg by a bullet. He had to be hospitalized. Once he was out of hospital and ready for duty, he requested that he be given the same job again. His request was granted, but unfortunately, he was shot at again and injured almost the way he had been earlier. He was hospitalized and when he was discharged from the hospital, he once again requested for the same duty. This shows how brave and committed the BSF are. When the home minister visited the site of the fencing work being done on the Jammu frontier, the head constable driver was presented before him. On my recommendation, he was awarded the Police Medal for Gallantry.

The strategy followed by the BSF was to excavate and build a mud wall during the night and put up the fence during the day. The idea was that the mud wall would provide protection to the men who were deployed to build the fence. In this manner, the fencing of this difficult frontier was completed. As a bonus, a ditch and mud wall, about a hundred kilometres long, were constructed and these could prove to be very useful for the army in times of war.

During my tenure, much of our efforts were devoted to curbing cross-border terrorism. Eventually, our efforts culminated in the elimination of Ghazi Baba, the man that many refer to as the Bin Laden of Kashmir.

GHAZI BABA MEETS HIS END

We became aware of a shadowy terrorist mastermind in Kashmir during the Delhi Police investigation of the attack on the Parliament. After the attack, our investigations revealed that the terrorists had instructed Afzal Guru that in case they died on the mission, their laptops should be handed over to their leader in Srinagar.

His name was Ghazi Baba.

This was the first time we'd heard his name. Immediately, a team of police officers was sent to Srinagar to investigate Ghazi Baba and, if possible, arrest him. Shockingly, nobody in any of the forces in Kashmir had even heard about him till then. As destiny would have it, I was transferred from the post of CP Delhi to the post of director general of the BSF. In my very first visit to Srinagar, I asked BSF officers what they knew about Ghazi Baba. Having orchestrated the investigation on the Parliament attack in Delhi, I was able to tell my officers all that we had learnt. I directed the Inspector General of the BSF in Srinagar to detail separate teams and make it their top priority to trace Ghazi Baba.

But the man was a shadow. How could we trace someone whose face had never been identified? It seemed that the BSF was waging a losing battle till they came across a cyclist who changed our destiny.

One morning, a man named Ansar Bhai was stopped at a BSF checkpost in Srinagar on his cycle. The nondescript fellow turned out to be a Pakistani national with connections with JeM, carrying several explosives! On interrogating him, we found that he knew of several hideouts of JeM. For quite some time, we had known that the people of downtown Srinagar were sheltering terrorists, either by choice or by force. During intensive interrogations of Ansar Bhai, we came to know of a mason who was an expert in making secret hideouts. One such house was identified in which the mason had recently built a secret room. Since this was a biggish building, it raised our suspicions.

It was the last week of August, and I was in Delhi attending a function. Whilst there, I received an urgent message.

There was a chance that Ghazi Baba was holed up in a safe house in an area known as Noor Bagh in Srinagar. I immediately sent a message to lay a siege on this house and evacuate all the residents from this building. Once the evacuation was complete, BSF men laid a cordon around the building. I also ordered that all the evacuated persons should be identified.

At about midnight, I got a report from the IG of BSF Srinagar. He informed me that he had planned to storm the building at 3 a.m., when all inside were likely to be asleep. When the men entered, there was a volley of gunfire. They retaliated. Balbir Singh, the wireless operator in the attacking BSF party, bore the brunt of the bullets and was martyred there and then. An attempt was made to enter the building with the help of two Assistant Commandants who were commandos. They tried to scale the building with ropes. The terrorists, who were inside, engaged in massive firing. One Assistant Commandant was grievously injured in the leg. He kept hanging from a rope because his leg had been seriously damaged. He could not have moved upward nor was he in a position to come down. It was then decided that he should be made to jump onto piled-up mattresses, which had been brought for the purpose. Achieving this feat was a near-impossible task. Fortunately, the injured officer was a trained commando, and he could perform this difficult job; he landed on the mattresses.

The BSF party then escalated its attack on the building and increased the intensity of firing. It was dark inside the building. The terrorists kept firing from inside. It was getting difficult for the BSF men to anticipate where the fire was coming from. The terrorists were also hurling grenades. One of them landed very close to where the BSF personnel were. Luckily, it did not explode, and no damage was done. The terrorists had the advantage of firing from the top. They could easily see the movement of the BSF men and decide how they could retaliate. It was turning out to be an unequal fight.

Incidentally, at this juncture, an assistant commandant decided to enter a room in which the militants were suspected to be. The room was very dark, but he could see a tall dressing table. He kicked this table a few times and lo and behold, it gave way to a secret door leading to another room. Ghazi Baba was hiding in this room and was about to be apprehended, but more firing came from inside the dark room. After an incessant round of brisk firing, the BSF managed to achieve its target. Ghazi Baba had been shot dead. His close associate had already been killed in an exchange of heavy fire a little earlier. However, during this fierce battle, the assistant commandant, who had kicked the dressing table, was hit by bullets and was grievously injured in his right hand because of which his rifle fell from his hand.

The next big challenge for the BSF party was to identify the dead body. In such high-profile cases, one must be doubly sure of the terrorist killed. Ghazi Baba was no ordinary terrorist. He was a cult figure for terrorists. His death would certainly have a telling effect on the JeM operating in Kashmir. Ghazi Baba's wife was also living with her newborn child in the same building in which he and his associates had been hiding. She had been moved from the building before the attack had been launched. The scene was quite dramatic as she came and was shocked to see the dead body of her husband. She broke down, started wailing and confirmed that the dead body was of Ghazi Baba.

As was expected, JeM denied that the BSF had killed Ghazi Baba. However, when the last rites were performed, thousands thronged the streets of Srinagar. There were slogans raised for him. He was called a *pir*, saint and a martyr. People shed tears incessantly and the mourners further confirmed that we had killed the right man, the man who was hailed by the terrorists as the Osama of Kashmir.

We received widespread accolades for this achievement. The BSF had successfully stalled the growth of JeM in Kashmir. Yet, something rankled.

It amazed me that in spite of the key role BSF had played in curtailing illegal cross-border activities and the success they had achieved against some of the most important terrorist leaders, they did not get the same appreciation as given to the Army. This had resulted in low morale amongst its men. During the Kargil War, I could see for myself the role the BSF was supposed to play during the war. But how could a force that perceived itself to be underrated and undervalued live up to its fullest potential?

CHANGING PERCEPTIONS, BOLSTERING THE FORCE

Conversations with BSF officers and the men at its far-flung outposts had revealed that they had good reason to feel dissatisfied and demoralized. Perhaps the sorest point among the officers was that the cadre review of the force had not taken place ever since the force had been raised. The cadre review is an exercise that helps estimate the requirements of new and additional posts. Without the cadre review, promotions had been stalled. While several new battalions had been raised, posts of gazetted officers had not been sanctioned along with them. A proposal for the sanction of cadre review, asking for the sanction of thousands of new posts had been sent a few years ago. Despite the efforts made by my predecessors to get it through, it had remained pending for about five years. The home secretary said that the finance ministry had not agreed to the proposal. The finance ministry would keep sending the file back with queries. While the two ministries played volleyball with the file, thousands of my young officers had almost given up hope for promotions.

As the head of the force, I took an appointment with the finance minister to apprise him of the facts. He was aghast. There and then, he called the concerned secretary. Within that week, about three thousand posts were sanctioned. It was the least I could do to raise the morale of these brave men for whom I had developed great respect.

There was another issue that had been pending for a long time. The BSF is the first line of defence of the country. Hence, training is its lifeline. Initially, twenty battalions were sanctioned as training reserve. This was done because every battalion is required to undergo an annual training of two months. But as the duties of BSF increased, the training of the battalions was being neglected. My predecessors had proposed the addition of twenty extra battalions. This, too, had been pending.

When I took over as the DG of the BSF, every time I met the home minister, I reminded him about sanctioning the twenty training battalions we had asked for. Eventually, just before I retired from service, the sanction orders for the twenty battalions were received. I felt that this was one of the most significant contributions I'd made to the force.

Many inequalities continued to exist. Often, jawans in border outposts would be troubled by the glaring differences in the facilities and allowances they received compared to what their peers in the Army got. They were right to feel slighted; there was no parity between the pay scales and facilities provided to both the forces. It was surprising that such differences should prevail. The dispensation of the government for both the services should have been the same. I took up the matter with the government and requested for parity in the scales for both.

So much so that when I visited our high altitude borders, I discovered that while army jawans received specialized high altitude clothing and diet, the kits and diets that

BSF men received were inferior in quality! After I made several representations, the scales for both these items were improved. This brought some solace to the officers and men of the BSF, but to my disappointment, the facilities given to the Army remained better than that of the BSF.

On 31 December 2004, I superannuated from the IPS. When I now reflect on the days I had spent in the BSF, I feel that BSF deserves more recognition for its stellar work in protecting our borders than it has received. To all those who don't agree, I invite them to spend one day in a BSF *jawan*'s shoes and see for themselves, the selfless heroism of their everyday lives!

EPILOGUE

Thirty-eight years in uniform is a long time. When I look back on these years, I marvel at the huge variety of experiences that they afforded me. Everything I know about life and living, I have learnt in uniform. Memories of the days policing mofussil districts slip and slide into myriad colourful patterns today, like the elements of a kaleidoscope. Today, as I sit in my quiet study and write these memoirs, a question keeps coming back to me. Was I a good officer?

A product of the times I lived and served in, I certainly did not do everything by the book. But could we have stopped lawless and violent criminals like Sriprakash Shukla and Sheodan Kachhi in their tracks by being sticklers for rules? I didn't think so then, and I don't think so now. I always respected the rulebook but never lost track of the fact that it had been made for the betterment of people—both in society and in the services. Rules have been made for us, not us for them. That is why in retrospect, I feel satisfied to look back on the numerous occasions when I reinterpreted the rulebook instead of blindly following it. For young officers joining the police today, this is perhaps the most heartfelt advice I can offer. Interrogate the rulebook, push against your boundaries and question your circumstances instead of simply accepting them. For only then will you succeed and be motivated to give your mental and physical best to the uniform you have pledged to serve.

When I look back, another thing I realize is that often the battles we lost taught me as much as the ones we won. And the times of waiting for the action to begin often taught me more about human nature, managing the force and strategizing, than the periods of intense action. To every young officer eager for action, I'd say, savour the quieter moments too, for they have a lot to teach. Policing is more of a waiting game than many would imagine.

The life of an Indian police officer is hard and mostly thankless. The job requires a missionary zeal and sacrifice. Perhaps that is why I have always advised young aspirants to wear the khaki only if they are genuinely passionate about it. The harsh realities of the job are such that unless one is totally committed, one simply cannot excel in it. At various points in my career, I have found similarities between the job of a police officer and that of a doctor. Under normal circumstances, an ordinary citizen would visit a doctor only when he is unwell. In the case of a police officer too, people would only visit him to report unpleasant incidents. Often, police officers find themselves overwhelmed by the negativity they have encountered in their jobs. I, for example, have not yet been able to banish the memory of my informant Lakhi lying dead with his eyes open—the man who died only because he was following my orders.

Yet, over the years, I've felt sorry to see that the police often do not enjoy a good image in the eyes of the public. Men in uniform must work much harder to acquire a public friendly image. Another painful observation I have made over the course of my career is that the police and especially paramilitary forces such as Border Security Force and Central Reserve Police Force have often not been seen at par with the military. Coming on top of the stresses of the job, this feeling of inequality and indeed, injustice, that too among men who are our first line of defence in the event of a war, needs to be urgently addressed.

Which is why, at the end of my innings, I asked myself why it is that in spite of it all, I have found my job so profoundly rewarding. As an officer who has had the privilege and honour of having been awarded two President's Police Medals for Gallantry, the Police Medal for Meritorious Service and the President's Police Medal for Distinguished Service, I can honestly say that there have been other things that have given me a greater sense of achievement. The satisfaction of bringing criminals to justice, the relief at having prevented a riot and the sheer excitement of the chase have been great motivators. But most of all, the respect and enduring goodwill of my men and the forces I have had the proud privilege of serving, is a medal that I wear till date with the greatest joy.

In the times ahead, I foresee an even greater role for the

police. The need of the hour is for it to constantly reinvent itself to meet the changing demands of society. It must gear up to solve cases of cybercrime, money laundering and terrorism—all very different from the sorts of crimes I solved in my time! As a career police officer, I feel that the crimes and criminals may change, but the role of the policeman will remain unchanged in importance. He is, and will always be, the only bulwark between chaos and order, between crime and the law. This is what I have believed in. This is what I have done since that momentous day, over half a century ago, when I decided to bite the bullet.

ACKNOWLEDGEMENTS

When I was first thinking of writing my memoir, I was unable to make up my mind to do so, as this thought came to my mind after about twelve years of my superannuation. When I discussed this idea with my wife Neerja Sharma, she was the person who encouraged me to write this book. Once I did begin writing this book, she kept motivating me throughout. But for her perhaps, this book would not have seen the light of day. I am really grateful to her for all her help.

My younger brother Professor L.R. Sharma, who headed the Department of English at the Allahabad University and is a writer himself, was a huge help to me. He kept on inspiring and goading me to complete the book. He lives in Allahabad but even if he came for a couple of days to stay with me, he would go to the extent of helping to type the manuscript for me. I would like to thank him for all the support he has given to me.

Geetanjali Krishna, my daughter-in-law, who is a

journalist by profession, is yet another person who motivated me a lot and kept assisting me in one thing or another. I especially appreciate her assistance for the pains she has taken in the tedious work of editing. I owe her my gratitude.

My younger daughter-in-law Anjali Bhardwaj, who is a social activist, has lent her support to me by giving new ideas while discussing some of the chapters with me. My thanks to her as well.

Reva Sharma, who is my niece and even though she lives in the UK, has taken a lot of interest in the writing of my book. She has not only inspired me but has taken the pain to edit some of the chapters of the book. I owe her a big thank you.

Without the help of Saurav Sinha, I would have taken much longer to finish this book than I have. His help, which I received whenever my computer developed a problem, was tremendous. Many thanks to him.

Last but not the least, I want to thank Rupa Publications for agreeing to publish my book and for all the help and guidance I got from them.